MUST JESUS BE LORD
TO BE SAVIOR?

By the same author:

THE CHURCH OF ROME AT THE BAR OF HISTORY

SALVATION, THE BIBLE AND ROMAN CATHOLICISM

THE CHRISTIAN: *WHAT IT MEANS TO KNOW AND FOLLOW CHRIST*

ROMAN CATHOLIC TRADITION: *CLAIMS AND CONTRADICTIONS*

PETER AND THE ROCK: *AN EXAMINATION OF THE PATRISTIC INTERPRETATION OF THE ROCK OF MATTHEW 16:18 AND OF THE EARLY CHURCH'S RELATIONHIP TO THE Bishops of Rome*

SAVING FAITH: *HOW DOES ROME DEFINE IT?*

MUST JESUS BE LORD
TO BE SAVIOR?

William Webster

CHRISTIAN RESOURCES INC.

CHRISTIAN RESOURCES INC.
304 W. T Street
Battle Ground, WA 98604

© *William Webster 1986, 1996*
First Published 1986
Second Printing 1996 – Revised and Updated

ISBN 1-789737-24-8

Printed and Bound in the United States

CONTENTS

Dedicated with deepest appreciation to Mr. Joseph Carroll and the staff of the Evangelical Institute of Greenville, S.C.

Introduction

This book was first published in 1986. Since that time there have been a number of works published addressing the issue of lordship salvation, most notably *The Gospel According to Jesus* by John MacArthur. However, there is still much confusion within the evangelical Church concerning this issue.

As I stated in the introduction to this book ten years ago there is much contradictory opinion as to what is necessary for an individual to come into the experience of salvation. On the one hand there are those who believe that lordship is absolutely essential while others deem such teaching a works salvation. No one involved in the controversy denies the essential truth of the deity of Christ, that he is Lord and God. In this sense it is impossible to 'make Christ Lord' since he *is* Lord. The controversy is not over the essential nature of Christ, but whether submission *to* him, as Lord of one's life, is a necessary aspect of saving faith. There are those who claim that lordship is a betrayal of the Reformation in that it undermines the vital reformation principle of 'faith alone'. And there are those who state that rather than a betrayal, the teaching of lordship is, in fact, an affirmation of both the biblical gospel and the historic Protestant faith. There is even confusion among those who consider themselves 'reformed' in theology. While we all agree that justification is by faith alone, we do not all agree on the meaning of saving faith. How do we resolve these differences?

I believe the answer is found both in clarifying the

discipleship teachings of the Lord Jesus Christ and in looking at the writings of the major evangelical theologians throughout the history of the Church. The teaching of Jesus is particularly germain to this whole controversy. What is the teaching of the Lord Jesus Christ? We must be able to hold our teaching of salvation and the gospel in integrity with the teaching of Jesus. If what we profess in any way conflicts with the teaching of Christ either by way of contradiction or omittance, we must humble ourselves, acknowledge our error and make whatever corrections are necessary to conform our teaching with his.

The controversy over lordship is not an academic issue. It hits right at the heart of the gospel and the meaning of true salvation. Nothing less than the eternal destiny of men and women is at stake. Consequently, this book is republished with the hope that the teachings of Christ and the historic teachings of evangelical theologians will clarify the issue regarding lordship salvation.

Chapter 1

The Nature of Sin

Bishop J.C. Ryle has made the comment that, 'a right knowledge of sin lies at the root of all saving Christianity.'[1] This is certainly true. Apart from a right understanding of sin, men cannot fully understand Christ's work of redemption, or the full meaning of repentance and faith. A superficial understanding of sin will automatically lead to a superficial repentance, resulting in a superficial Christianity. Therefore it is vitally importance to clearly define the nature of sin in order to clearly define the nature of repentance. It is for this purpose that the following quotes are given from leading conservative evangelical theologians on the nature of sin.

J.I. Packer

The words which our Bibles translate as 'sin' in both Old and New Testaments, mean either failing to hit a target or reach a standard, or failing to obey authority. And the standard unreached, the target missed, the path abandoned, the law transgressed, the authority defied, are in each case God's. God, and His will, are the measure of sin.

Sin is turning out of the way He has commanded (Ex. 32:8) into a forbidden way of your own (Isa. 53:6). Sin is going contrary to God, retreating from God, turning one's back on God, defying God, ignoring God.

What in positive terms is the essence of sin? Playing God; and as a means to this, refusing to allow the Creator to be God so far as you are concerned. Living, not for Him, but for yourself; loving and serving and pleasing yourself without reference to the Creator, trying to be as far as possible independent of Him, taking yourself out of His hands, holding Him at arm's length, keeping the reins of life in your own hands; acting as if you, and your pleasure, were the end to which all things else, God included, must be made to function as a means—That is the attitude in which sin essentially consists.

Sin is exalting oneself against the Creator, withholding the homage due to Him, and putting oneself in His place, as the ultimate standard of reference in all life's decisions . . . **where Christ does not rule sin does.**[2]

John Stott

Sin is more than an unfortunate outward act or habit, it is a deep seated inward corruption. In fact, the sins we commit are merely outward and visible manifestations of this inward and invisible malady, the symptoms of a moral disease.

Sin is a tendency or bias of self–centeredness which we inherit, which is rooted deeply in our human personality and which manifests itself in a thousand ugly ways. Sin lies at the root of our personality. It controls our ego. In fact, sin is self. All the sins we commit are assertions of the self against either God or man. God's order is that we put Him first, others next, self last. Sin is the reversal of the order. It is to put ourselves first, our neighbor next and God somewhere in the background.[3]

Henry C. Thiessen

Sin is essentially selfishness. Scripture teaches that the
essence of godliness is love of God. Is not the essence of sin
the love of self? Each of us has turned to his own way (Isa.
53:6). What we mean is such an exaggerated love of self as
puts self interest ahead of God's interests. That selfishness
is the essence of sin is evident also from the fact that all the
forms of sin can be traced to selfishness as their source.
Thus man's natural appetites, his sensuality, selfish
ambitions and selfish affections are rooted in his
selfishness.

Jesus exemplified true unselfishness. He said, 'I do not
seek my own will but the will of Him Who sent Me' (John
5:30).

Paul regarded love as the fulfillment of the law (Rom. 13:
10). He said that Christ died for all that they who live
should no longer live for themselves but for Him Who died
and rose again on their behalf (2 Cor. 5:15) and he
represents people in the last days as being lovers of self (2
Tim. 3:2).

These and other Scriptures represent selfishness as the
essence of sin—the principle from which all else springs.[4]

W.E. Vine

'Anomia'—lawlessness, iniquity. I John 3:4—Sin is
lawlessness.

In 1 John 3:4 the R.V. adheres to the real meaning of the
word, 'everyone that doeth sin (a practice, not the
committal of an act) doeth also lawlessness: and sin is
lawlessness.' This definition of sin sets forth its essential
character as the rejection of the law, or will of God, and the
substitution of the will of self.[5]

Augustus H. Strong

We hold the essential principle of sin to be selfishness. By selfishness we mean not simply the exaggerated self-love which constitutes the antithesis of benevolence, but that choice of self as the supreme end which constitutes the antithesis of supreme love to God. That selfishness is the essence of sin may be shown as follows: Love to God is the essence of all virtue. The opposite to this, the choice of self as the supreme end must therefore be the essence of sin...to make our own happiness our ultimate aim is itself sin and the essence of sin. As God makes His holiness the central thing, so we are to live for that, loving self only in God and for God's sake. This love for God as holy is the essence of virtue. The opposite to this, or supreme love for self is sin. The sinner raises some lower object of instinct or desire to supremacy, regardless of God and His law, and this he does for no other reason than to gratify self...All the different forms of sin can be shown to have their root in selfishness, while selfishness itself, considered as the choice of self as a supreme end, cannot be resolved into any simpler elements.

Sin therefore is not merely a negative thing, or an absence of love to God. It is a fundamental and positive choice or preference of self instead of God, as the object of affection and the supreme end of being. **Instead of making God the center of his life, surrendering himself unconditionally to God and possessing himself only in subordination to God's will, the sinner makes self the center of his life,** sets himself directly against God and constitutes his own interest the supreme motive and his own will the supreme rule.

While sin as a state is unlikeness to God, as a principle is opposition to God and as an act is transgression of God's law, the essence of it always and everywhere is selfishness. It is therefore, not something external, or the result of compulsion from without; it is a depravity of the affections and a perversion of the will, which constitutes man's inmost character. Sin is essentially egoism or selfism, putting self in God's place. It has four principle characteristics or manifestations:

1. Self sufficiency instead of faith.
2. Self will instead of submission.
3. Self seeking instead of benevolence or love.
4. Self righteousness instead of humility and reverence.

Sin is a state, a state of will, a selfish state of the will.[6]

Jonathan Edwards

The apostacy of man summarily consists in departing from the true God, to idols; forsaking his Creator, and setting up other things in his room. When God at first created man, he was united to his Creator; the God that made him was his God. The true God was the object of his highest respect, and had the possession of his heart. Love to God was the principle in his heart, that ruled over all other principles; and everything in the soul was wholly in subjection to it. But when man fell, he departed from the true God, and the union that was between his heart and his Creator was broken: he wholly lost his principle of love to God. And henceforth man clave to other gods. He gave that respect to the creature, which is due to the Creator. When God ceased to be the object of his supreme love and respect, other things of course became the objects of it.

Man will necessarily have something that he respects as his god. If man does not give his highest respect to the God that made him, there will be something else that has the possession of it. Men will either worship the true God, or some idol: it is impossible that it should be otherwise: something will have the heart of man. And that which a man gives his heart to, may be called his god: and therefore when man by the fall extinguished all love to the true God, he set up the creature in his room. For having lost his esteem and love of the true God, and set up other gods in his room, and in opposition to him; and God still demanding their worship, and opposing them; enmity necessarily follows.

That which a man chooses for his god, he sets his heart mainly upon. And nothing will so soon excite enmity, as opposition in that which is dearest. A man will be the greatest enemy to him who opposes him in what he chooses for his god: he will look on none as standing so much in his way, as he that would deprive him of his god...A man in this respect cannot serve two masters, that stand in competition for his service. And not only, if he serves one, he cannot serve the other; but if he cleaves to one, he will necessarily hate the other. Matt. 6:24, 'No man can serve two masters; for either he will hate the one, and love the other, or else he will hold to the one, and despise the other. Ye cannot serve God and mammon.' And this is the very reason that men hate God. In this case it is, as when two kings set up in one kingdom, in opposition one to the other; and they both challenge the same throne, and are competitors for the same crown: they who are loyal, hearty subjects to the one, will necessarily be enemies to the other. As that which is a man's god, is the object of his highest love; so that God who chiefly opposes him in it, must be the object of his greatest hatred.

The gods which a natural man worships, instead of the God that made him, are himself and the world. He has withdrawn his esteem and honour from God, and proudly exalts himself. As Satan was not willing to be in subjection; and therefore rebelled, and set up himself; so a natural man, in the proud and high thoughts he has of himself, sets up himself upon God's throne. He gives his heart to the world, worldly riches, worldly pleasures, and worldly honours: they have the possession of that regard which is due to God. The apostle sums up all the idolatry of wicked men in their love of the world. 1 John 2:15,16, 'Love not the world, neither the things that are in the world. If any man

love the world, the love of the Father is not in him. For all
that is in the world, the lust of the flesh, the lust of the eye,
and the pride of life, is not of the Father, but is of the world.'
And the apostle James observes that a man must
necessarily be the enemy of the true God, if he be a friend
of the world. 'Whosoever therefore will be a friend of the
world, is the enemy of God' (James 4:4)...Natural men are
enemies to God, because he is so opposite to them, in that
in which they place their all...to that in which natural men
place all their delight, and all their happiness.[7]

Summation

The essence of sin is not centered primarily in acts of sinful
external behavior but in self–will, self–rule, or selfishness.
It is living for self. Living a self–centered, self–directed life
for the fulfillment of personal interests and ambitions
rather than for God and his interests. One's life, in other
words, is dominated and controlled by self.

As Dr. Thiessen points out, the Bible sums up the essence
of sin very concisely in Isaiah 53:6: 'All we like sheep have
gone astray, we have turned every one to his own way.'

Now that we have clearly defined the essence and nature
of sin it is possible to discuss in a meaningful way the nature
of repentance.

Chapter 2

The Necessity for and Nature of Repentance

In this chapter we will address the nature of repentance and its place in the scheme of salvation. What will be shown biblically is that, given the nature of sin, submission to the Lordship of Christ is the essence of true repentant faith and is therefore necessary for salvation.

First it is important to realize that the Bible presents repentance as a separate and distinct concept from faith. They are two completely different Greek words, and they mean entirely different things, though in the experience of salvation or conversion, they may seem to be indivisible. J.I. Packer writes, 'The gospel is a summons to faith and repentance. All who hear the gospel are summoned by God to repent and believe (Acts 17:30, John 6:29). Faith and repentance are both acts, and acts of the whole man.'[8] John Calvin makes the following comment: 'The sum of the gospel is held to consist in repentance and forgiveness of sins (Luke 24:47, Acts 5:31). Any discussion of faith, therefore, that omitted these two topics would be barren and mutilated and well nigh useless.'[9]

That repentance is necessary for salvation but is used as a separate concept from faith is seen in the following verses:

Thus it is written, that the Christ should suffer, and rise again from the dead the third day; and that **repentance** for forgiveness of sins should be proclaimed in His name to all nations, beginning from Jerusalem (Luke 24:46-47).

Jesus came into Galilee, preaching the gospel of God, and saying, 'The time is fulfilled, and the kingdom of God is at hand: **repent** and believe in the gospel' (Mark 1: 14,15).

Unless you **repent,** you will all likewise perish (Luke 13:3).

Therefore having overlooked the times of ignorance, God is now declaring to men that all everywhere should **repent** (Acts 17:30).

I did not shrink from declaring to you anything that was profitable, and teaching you publicly and from house to house, solemnly testifying to both Jews and Greeks of **repentance** toward God and faith in our Lord Jesus Christ (Acts 20:20,21).

The Lord is not...wishing for any to perish, but for all to come to **repentance** (2 Peter 3:9).

The word of God clearly states that repentance and faith are both necessary for salvation. Delete either one and you do not have biblical salvation or a biblical gospel.

Faith without repentance cannot save because the Lord Jesus clearly says, 'Except ye repent ye will all likewise perish' (Luke 13:3). And repentance without faith cannot save because it is faith that justifies. Therefore we must conclude that salvation is the result of repentant faith. Both must be present.

It is also important to note that this call to repentance is not to be understood as something which applies only to the Jews in a different dispensation. The Lord Jesus commanded that it be preached as a part of the great commission to the whole world (Luke 24:44) and Paul in summing up the gospel that he preached to both Gentiles and Jews (Acts 20:19-20) said it consisted of repentance toward God and faith in the Lord Jesus Christ.

Since repentance is necessary for salvation, what exactly is biblical repentance? In other words, if an individual is going to repent, what is that going to mean? How is this truth to be applied? The Bible answers this in the teaching of the Lord Jesus Christ.

What does Jesus teach about salvation and the requirements for entering the kingdom of God? Let's examine the scriptures.

CHRIST'S CALL TO DISCIPLESHIP

In Luke 14, Jesus gives the following conditions of discipleship:

> If anyone comes to Me, and does not hate his own father and mother and wife and children and brothers and sisters, yes, and even his own life, he cannot be my disciple (Lk. 14:26).

> Whoever does not carry his own cross and come after Me cannot be My disciple (Lk. 14:27).

> So therefore, no one of you can be My disciple who does not give up all his own possessions (Lk. 14:33).

It is clear that Jesus is not talking here about a process of discipleship, but a *commitment* of discipleship. While a biblical commitment to Christ results in a process of growth, in this particular passage Christ is talking about an initial commitment to himself. Jesus has enunciated unalterable and absolute requirements which he says must be met or one cannot become his disciple. Let us examine his words to see what exactly the Lord means by his

21

teaching.

1.) Luke 14:26: 'If anyone comes to Me, and does not hate his own father and mother and wife and children and brothers and sisters, yes, and even his own life, he cannot be My disciple.'

To properly interpret the meaning of the Lord's words, especially his use of the word hate, we need to refer to Matthew 10:37: 'He who loves father or mother more than Me is not worthy of Me; he who loves son or daughter more than Me is not worthy of Me.'

What Jesus is dealing with here is love and devotion. Jesus demands first place in the heart of an individual. He must be preeminent in the life. All other relationships are to take a secondary place in relationship to himself. William Hendriksen makes the following comments on this verse:

> He tells the people that devotion to Himself must be so wholehearted that even attachment to parents and to other members of one's family must not be allowed to stand in the way. Clearly the meaning of the word hate in the Lucan passage is to love less. In all things Christ must always have the preeminence (Col 1:18). That the word hate in Luke 14:26 cannot have the meaning which we generally attach to it is clear also from the fact that Jesus tells us to love even our enemies (Matt 5:44). What the Savior demands in Luke 14:26 and other passages is complete devotion, the type of loyalty that is so true and unswerving that every other attachment, even to one's own life must be subjected to it. If a person is unwilling to tender that unconditional devotion, then says Jesus, 'he cannot be My disciple.'[10]

2.) Luke 14:27: 'Whoever does not carry his own cross and come after Me cannot be My disciple.'

The issue in this verse is that of self denial. We will be

looking at this concept in more detail but these words by G. Campbell Morgan adequately sum up what the Lord Jesus means:

> What is self denial?. . .To deny self is to say no to every wish that comes out of the personal life. To deny self is radical. It goes down to the roots of things. A man may practice self denial all his life and never deny himself. A man may practice self denial in this and that respect, and all the while his self–centeredness is strengthened. Jesus did not say exercise self denial in externalities. He said deny self, have done with choosing, wishing, planning, arranging for self. Choose no more, will no more, except to will that God shall will...I deny self when I hand over the keys of the citadel to the king and say, Enter and reign in every chamber of the being, in all possibilities of the soul.[11]

So, Jesus must not only be first in one's affections, but his will must come first in one's life. An individual's will must be submitted to the will of Jesus Christ.

3.) Luke 14:33: 'So therefore, no one of you can be My disciple who does not give up all his own possessions.'
William Hendriksen states, 'Wholehearted devotion, all–out loyalty, complete self denial, so that one places himself, his time, his earthly possessions, his talents etc., at the disposal of Christ, is what Jesus asks.'[12]
As a matter of summation, then, what Jesus is calling for in these verses is a forsaking of everything and the unconditional surrender of self to him as Lord if we are to become his disciple. These are the conditions he clearly sets forth for entering into a relationship with himself. It is a commitment that is necessary for entering the kingdom of God. Apart from this commitment to become his disciple we cannot be saved.
In order to show this is an accurate interpretation of

Jesus' teaching in Luke 14 it is essential that we look carefully at a number of additional passages that deal with Jesus' teaching on discipleship. These are Mark 8:34-37, John 12:24-26, Matthew 11:28-30 and Mark 10:17-22. These passages reveal three general word pictures used by Jesus which are descriptive of his teaching on salvation and discipleship: the cross, the yoke and the grain of wheat. They each illustrate the attitude towards self we must adopt if we are to be rightly related to him. They teach us that a Christian is one who has died to his life, in this world, and given himself wholly to Christ, to love him supremely and serve him exclusively. We cannot follow Christ and possess eternal life unless these word pictures are descriptive of our lives.

Mark 8:34-37: The Cross

> If anyone wishes to come after Me, let him deny himself, and take up his cross, and follow Me. For whoever wishes to save his life shall lose it; but whoever loses his life for My sake and the gospel's shall save it. For what does it profit a man to gain the whole world, and forfeit his soul? For what shall a man give in exchange for his soul? (Mk. 8:34–37. Cf. Lk. 9:23–27).

This is another foundational passage related to discipleship. In fact, Mark 8:34 is in principle the same verse as Luke 14:27. But in Mark 8 Jesus amplifies the verse, so we will understand exactly what he means. Whatever it means in Mark 8:34 is what it means in Luke 14:27.

These words of Jesus to his disciples and the multitudes follow the incident of Peter's attempt to dissuade the Lord from the path of the cross. Peter appeals to him to spare himself. Peter's admonition springs from loving concern, but it is met with a stern, severe rebuke from Jesus. His reply to Peter is both revealing and instructive for it reveals to us the master principle that governed the life of Christ. And it is this initial response to Peter which forms the backdrop to his additional comments to all the disciples and the multitudes. Jesus utterly rejects Peter's suggestion, actually ascribing it to Satan, and then says to Peter: 'You are not setting your mind on God's interests, but man's (Mk. 8:33).' Here Jesus sets forth a contrast between two life principles: God's interests and man's interests. And he reveals that the two are in conflict with one another. But he leaves us in no doubt as to which principle dominated his life. Jesus was controlled by one master passion: To know and do the will of God no matter what the cost to himself. Jesus' life was not governed by his own interests, but those of his Father's. As he himself stated over and over again: 'For I have come down from heaven, not to do My own will, but the will of Him who sent Me' (Jn. 6:38). Self interest is the very antithesis of the life of Christ. His one holy passion was the will of God, for the glory of God, even if it meant persecution, suffering and death on a cross!

There is the stark contrast here between man's interests and God's interests. It forms the context in which Jesus teaches about the cross and what it means to follow him. Being his follower means adopting the same attitude towards my life that he had towards his. After calling the multitudes and the disciples to himself Jesus says that if any man would come after him he must do three things: deny himself, take up his cross, and follow him. What does this mean?

Deny self: This means a turning from self–will, renouncing living for self. John Stott says: 'Self denied...is not to deny things to myself, but to deny myself to myself. It is to say no to self and yes to Christ; to repudiate self and acknowledge Christ.'[13]

Take up the cross : A cross is an instrument of death and is used in a metaphorical sense by Jesus. When the term is used in conjunction with the phrase 'deny self', it carries the idea of dying to my right to myself and of living to promote my own interests. John Stott comments: 'To take up a cross is to put oneself into the position of a condemned man on his way to execution. In other words, the attitude to self is that of crucifixion. Everyday the Christian is to die. Everyday he renounces the sovereignty to his own will. Everyday he renews his unconditional surrender to Jesus Christ.'[14]

Follow me: The tense of this verb indicates that it means to continually follow. Thayer's *Greek English Lexicon of the New Testament* states that the Greek word follow means 'to join one as a disciple, to become or be his disciple.' To follow Jesus therefore means a death to self to become his disciple. I cease to live for my sake in order that I might live for his sake.

Why the imperative call to deny self, take up a cross and follow Jesus? *'For'*, he says, 'whosoever will save his life shall *lose* it, but whosoever shall lose his life for my sake and the gospel's the same shall save it' (Mk. 8:35). The key to understanding the meaning of this verse is the word *lose*. The Greek 'lose' is precisely the same Greek word that is translated *perish* in other parts of the New Testament. It means to die eternally:

The Lord is not...wishing for any to perish, but for all to come to **repentance** (2 Peter 3:9).

For God so loved the world, that he gave his only begotten Son, that whoever believes in Him should not *perish*, but have eternal life (Jn. 3:16).

To insure that we fully understand the issues involved Christ further explains and emphasizes his point in verses

36-37:

> For what does it profit a man to gain the whole world, and forfeit his soul? For what shall a man give in exchange for his soul?

Jesus is saying that if a man does not deny self, take up a cross and commit to be his follower or disciple then that man will *perish*—he will forfeit his soul. Jesus makes this same point in John 10:27-28 where he once again uses the word 'follow' as a characteristic of his sheep:

> My sheep hear My voice, and I know them, and they *follow* Me; and I give eternal life to them, and they shall never perish; and no one shall snatch them out of My hand.

Who are the true sheep of the Lord Jesus? Who are the ones who hear his voice, to whom he gives eternal life and who will therefore never perish? It is those who *follow* him; those who commit themselves to him to become his disciples. The issue is one of eternity and salvation. Both William Hendriksen and R.C.H. Lenski make this point in their comments on Mark 8:34:

> This is not self denial in the current sense of the word but *true conversion*, the very first essential of the Christian life.[15]

> Together the three (deny self, take up a cross, and follow me) indicate true conversion followed by a life long sanctification.[16]

Based upon the meaning and contextual interpretation of the words Jesus used one can only conclude that Mark 8:34 is stating a requirement for salvation. This scripture clearly says that one cannot become a Christian without a commitment to Christ as a disciple. In Luke 14:27, the parallel passage to Mark 8:34, Jesus also relates discipleship to salvation. In Mark 8 Jesus says one must become his disciple or he will perish. In Luke 14 he amplifies for us the conditions which must be fulfilled if one would become his disciple. It is obvious from our study of the above passage that when Jesus uses the term 'disciple', he uses it as a synonym for the term Christian. To become a disciple, therefore, is to become a Christian. To become a Christian is to become a disciple. Thus, the whole passage in Luke 14 is the setting forth of his conditions for entering the kingdom of God. William Hendriksen's comments on the importance of obeying Christ's demands in Mark 8:34 and Luke 9:23 to deny self and take up a cross are worth noting:

> In the next three verses...the obligation to be converted, etc., and the reward that results are brought into sharp contrast with the loss experienced by those who refuse to deny themselves, to take up their cross, and to follow Jesus...Accordingly, with an implied 'Let him not refuse,' there follows...For whoever would save his life shall lose it, but whoever loses his life for my sake, he shall save it. Meaning: the individual who would—or 'should wish to'—save his life shall lose it. Exactly what is it that he wishes to save? Answer: his life, that is, himself...This man clings to that sinful life of his, holding on to it tenaciously...On the other hand, whoever loses his life 'for my sake,' he shall save it. One loses his life in the present sense by devoting oneself completely to Christ, to the service of those in need, to the gospel (Cf. Mark 8:35). Note that Christ lays claim to absolute devotion. This proves that he regards himself as Lord of all, and that the evangelist was fully aware of this! The person who offers this devotion saves his life, that is, his soul, or as we can also say, *himself*...It is only by losing oneself—looking away from self in order to serve

the Master and his 'little ones' (Cf. Matt. 25:40)—that one can ever be saved...For the sinner salvation is impossible apart from obedience to this rule.[17]

In light of these passages it is clear that Jesus never taught that an individual could become a Christian and then at a later time make a secondary wholehearted commitment to him as a disciple. Jesus does not separate being a Christian from being a disciple. They are interchangeable terms. According to Jesus, if one is not a disciple he is not a Christian. When he calls men to himself to be saved he calls them to a discipleship commitment—to the taking up of a cross to crucify self to become a follower. And scripture teaches that all who truly belong to Christ have done that: 'Now those who belong to Christ Jesus have crucified the flesh with its passions and desires' (Gal. 5:24). There are a number of other examples which amplify and highlight this emphasis in the teaching and evangelism of Jesus.

Matthew 11:28-30: The Yoke

Come to Me, all who are weary and heavy–laden, and I will give you rest. Take My yoke upon you, and learn from Me, for I am gentle and humble in heart; and you shall find rest for your souls. For My yoke is easy, and My load is light.

In Mark 8 and Luke 14 Jesus uses the image of the cross to communicate the conditions of discipleship. Here he refers to a yoke. What does Jesus mean by his yoke? In Jewish culture the yoke was used to harness animals, to control them and bring them into submission to one's will, so that they could be used in labor. In this passage (Mt. 11), Jesus issues an invitation to men to come to him to find rest for their souls. He sets forth an invitation, a condition and a promise. The invitation is 'come to me'. The promise is rest and the condition is 'take my yoke upon you.'

Man is restless and burdened. Why? Because he is ruled by self and not by God. What Jesus is saying is that he can give us rest but it requires a certain kind of commitment. We must bend our necks under his yoke and come into submission to his authority and teaching. We must be willing to adopt the same heart towards self that Jesus himself has. He tells us in this passage that he is meek and humble in heart. His whole life is dominated and governed by God and his will and interests. If we would come to him and find rest we must repudiate self and selfish interests and submit ourselves to Jesus as Lord—to yield to his yoke, his authority and control. James Montgomery Boice makes these observations on the meaning of Christ's yoke:

> In one of Jesus' most important sayings about discipleship...the Lord pictures discipleship as putting on a yoke. This suggests a number of things, but chiefly it suggests submission to Christ for His assigned work. It is the picture of an animal yoked to others as well as to a plow.
>
> A yoke is also the connection between submission and subjection. 'Submit' comes from the two Latin words *sub* (meaning 'under') and *mitto, mittere* (meaning 'to put' or 'place'). So submission means putting oneself under the authority of another. 'Subject' also comes from two Latin words, in this case *sub* (meaning 'under') and *iacto, iactare* (meaning 'cast' or 'throw'). It means being put under the authority of another. In other words, although the first word has an active sense (I put myself under another's authority) and the second word has a passive sense (I am placed under that authority), the idea is nevertheless essentially the same. Moreover, it is connected with 'yoke' in this way. In ancient times it was customary for a ruler, when he had conquered a new people or territory, to place a staff across two upright poles, perhaps four feet off the ground, and require the captured people to pass under it.

By this act they passed under his yoke or submitted to his authority. When Jesus used this image He was saying that to follow Him was to submit to Him. It was to receive Him as Lord of one's life.[18]

John 12:24-26: The Grain of Wheat

Truly, truly, I say to you, unless a grain of wheat falls into the earth and dies, it remains by itself alone; but if it dies it bears much fruit. He who loves his life loses it; and he who hates his life in this world shall keep it to life eternal. If anyone serves Me, let him follow Me; and where I am, there shall My servant also be; if anyone serves Me, the Father will honor him.

Jesus gives us yet another word picture here which is descriptive of both his own life and that of the Christian. Again he is illustrating what it means to come into a saving relationship with himself. First of all, he depicts himself as a grain of wheat in describing his death on the cross. He is using a principle drawn from the physical world to teach a spiritual truth. What is that truth? Fruitfulness and life is born out of death. It is only as the grain of wheat falls into the ground and dies that it produces fruit. Just so, unless the Son of Man goes to the cross there will be no fruit, but if he dies there will be much spiritual fruit for the kingdom of God.

Through this word picture Jesus tells us the attitude he has towards his own life. His life is not lived unto himself but totally for the sake of others—first and foremost for his Father and then for people. He constantly gives of himself even to the point of death.

Jesus then applies this principle to all who would be his followers. He says there are two fundamental attitudes that we can adopt towards our life in this world: that of love and that of hatred. Jesus says that if we love our life we will lose it, but if we hate it we will keep it to life eternal. We must understand the word hate here in the same way that Jesus used it in Luke 14. He means that nothing is to take priority over himself and the kingdom of God in our hearts. Everything else is to be *loved less*. Our lives are not to be our highest priority. We are not here to live for ourselves but for our Lord. We are not to literally hate ourselves but our love for God and his kingdom must take absolute priority over our lives. If we love our life more than Christ we will lose it. This word *lose* is the same word Jesus uses in Mark 8 which means to perish. He is speaking here about eternal death and eternal life.

He then states that to be his servant we must *follow* him. If we would gain *eternal life* and truly know Christ there must be a death to self. I must become, in a figurative sense, a grain of wheat which falls into the ground and dies. I must come to an end of living for myself and this world. I commit myself unreservedly to Christ to be his follower—to love him supremely and to serve him exclusively. If I do not do this Jesus says I will perish. He says the same thing in Mark 8. We die to ourselves that we might live for God and his will and the result is fruit. The apostle Paul writes of this in Romans 12:1 where he exhorts believers to continually offer themselves to God as a living sacrifice: 'I urge you therefore brethren by the mercies of God to present your bodies a living and holy sacrifice, acceptable to God, which is your spiritual service of worship.' F.F. Bruce makes these comments on the meaning of Jesus' teaching about the grain of wheat in John 12:24:

> The principle stated in verse 24 is of wide application; in particular, if it is true of Jesus, it must be true of his followers. They too must be prepared to renounce present interests for the sake of a future inheritance. This is a Johannine counterpart to the Synoptic saying about the disciple's obligation to take up his cross and follow his

Master (cf. Mark 8:34-38). To love one's life here means to give it priority over the interests of God's kingdom; similarly to hate one's life is to give priority over it to the interests of God's kingdom.[19]

The New Testament scholar, D.A. Carson, gives these insightful and sobering observations in explaining the essence of Jesus' teaching:

But if the principle modelled by the seed—that death is the necessary condition for the generation of life—is peculiarly applicable to Jesus, in a slightly different way it is properly applied to all of Jesus' followers...The movement of thought in this passage runs from Jesus' uniquely fruitful death (the death of one seed producing many living seeds) to the mandated death of Jesus' followers as the necessary condition of their *own* life. The person who *loves his own life will lose it*: it could not be otherwise, for to love one's life is a fundamental denial of God's sovereignty, of God's rights, and a brazen elevation of self to the apogee of one's perception, and therefore an idolatrous focus on self, which is the heart of all sin. Such a person loses his life, *i.e.* causes his own perdition. By contrast, the one *who hates his life* (the love/hate contrast reflects a semitic idiom that articulates fundamental preference, not hatred on some absolute scale...) *will keep it for eternal life* (*cf.* Mk. 8:35 par...). This person denies himself, or, to use another of Jesus' metaphors, takes up his cross daily (Mk. 8:34 par.), *i.e.* he chooses not to pander to self–interest but at the deepest level of his being declines to make himself the focus of his interest and perception, thereby *dying*.

A second contrast emerges in v. 25. The man who hates his life *in this world* will keep it *for eternal life*...These choices cannot be acts of mere self–abnegation. Self must be displaced by another; the endless, shameless focus on self must be displaced by focus on Jesus Christ, who is the supreme revelation of God.[20]

The theme of Jesus' teaching in John 12 is that of fruit. This is an important theme throughout the New Testament:

- Romans 7:4 states that a believer is united to Christ with the ultimate purpose of bearing fruit unto God.
- In John 12 Jesus defines what conditions are necessary for union with Christ to take place that fruit might be produced: a death to self with a corresponding commitment to Christ to be his follower or disciple.
- John 15:8 says that we are to bear much fruit and so *prove* to be Christ's disciple. Only a disciple can bear fruit. And a true disciple is one who has met the conditions set forth by Jesus in Luke 14, Mark 8, Matthew 11 and John 12.
- Romans 6:22 states that fruit can only come from a heart and life that is wholly consecrated to God .

Discipleship is the essence of true Christianity. All who would come into the kingdom of God must submit their lives to Christ as his disciple to be his follower. This is evident in the commission that Christ gives to his disciples in Matthew 28:19-20 in the preaching of the gospel:

All authority in heaven and hearth has been given to Me. Go therefore and make disciples of all nations, baptizing them in the name of the Father and the Son and the Holy Spirit, teaching them to observe all that I commanded you, And lo I am with you always even to the end of the age.

This passage of scripture is known as the Great Commission. It is the Savior's commission to his followers to go into all the world and 'make disciples.'

The Lord himself has already defined the word disciple in

34

Luke 14. Therefore the word is going to retain the same
meaning in Matthew 28. He is commissioning his followers
to carry on the same ministry he has been engaged in—that
of bringing men and women to himself through the
preaching of the gospel. To 'make disciples' is to bring men
and women to the kind of commitment that is defined by
Jesus in Luke 14. Such people then become disciples or true
converts. Then we are told to baptize *them* and teach
them. Who does the word *them* refer to? Clearly to those
who have been 'made disciples'. We are to baptize and then
teach those who have been become disciples. This passage
is not dealing only with a process of growth in discipleship,
but with that point of commitment where an individual
becomes a true follower of the Lord Jesus Christ. The Lord
is commissioning his disciples to carry on the same kind of
evangelism he has been involved in throughout his
ministry. One clear example of this is seen in the incident
of the rich young ruler.

The Rich Young Ruler

> And as He was setting out on a journey, a man ran up to
> Him and knelt before Him and began asking Him, 'Good
> teacher, what shall I do to inherit eternal life?' And Jesus
> said to him, 'Why do you call Me good? No one is good
> except God alone. You know the commandments, Do not
> murder, Do not commit adultery, Do not steal, Do not
> bear false witness, Do not defraud, Honor your father and
> mother.' And he said to him, 'Teacher I have kept all these
> things from my youth up.'
>
> And looking at him, Jesus felt a love for him, and said to
> him, 'One thing you lack: go and sell all you possess and
> give to the poor and you shall have treasure in heaven, and
> come follow Me.' But at these words his face fell and he
> went away grieved, for he was one who owned much
> property (Mk. 10:17-22).

This passage of scripture is very important as it relates to our present study. This man comes to Jesus earnestly seeking the way of eternal life. He specifically asks the Lord what he must do to be saved. And Jesus tells him that he lacks one thing. He must sell all he possesses, give the proceeds to the poor, and follow him. Again we are confronted with this key word—*follow*. This is the same condition Jesus lays before the multitudes in Luke 14: 'Whoever does not take up his cross and *follow Me* cannot be My disciple...No one of you can be My disciple who does not give up all his own possessions' (Lk. 14:27,33). The Lord places this condition before the young ruler as a condition for salvation. If he would enter the kingdom of God and inherit eternal life he must forsake all and follow Christ. As we have already seen the word 'follow' means to become a disciple. He can gain eternal life if he is willing to become a disciple. This means unreserved surrender to Christ as Lord. Walter Chantry makes the following comments:

> Often Christ turned crowds away by insisting that 'whosoever he be of you that forsaketh not all that he hath, he cannot be My disciple' (Lk. 14:33). He was not speaking of abundant life nor of 'victorious' giants of the faith...He demanded this turning from everything to himself as a condition of discipleship for everyone. The young ruler would turn from earthly riches to heavenly or he would cling to earthly riches and perish...The sinner must know that Jesus will not be a Savior to any man who refuses to bow to him as Lord...Christ knew nothing of the man-made twentieth-century suggestion that taking Jesus as Lord is optional. For him it was no second step which is essential for great blessings but unnecessary for entering God's kingdom. The altered message of today has deceived men and women by convincing them that Jesus

will gladly be a Savior even to those who refuse to follow him as Lord. It simply is not the truth! Jesus' invitation to salvation is, 'Come, follow me'...Practical acknowledgment of Jesus' Lordship, yielding to his rule by following is the very fibre of saving faith...Believing is obeying. Without obedience, you shall not see life! Unless you bow to Christ's scepter you will not receive the benefits of Christ's sacrifice. That is just what Jesus said to the ruler.[21]

Christ preached the law to the rich young ruler to bring him under conviction and to repentance. He put his finger on the young man's idol and demanded a forsaking of that idol if he would inherit eternal life. Jesus did not tell the rich young ruler simply to 'believe' in him. He commanded him to become a disciple. This is Jesus' message in evangelism, a call to discipleship. Thus, in Matthew 28:18–20 he is commissioning his disciples to follow his example.

It is clear from these passages that Christ taught that salvation requires a commitment to him as Lord. To understand why this is true we need to understand how Jesus' teaching relates to the gospel message itself.

JESUS' DEFINITION OF THE WORD DISCIPLE

The yoke, the cross, the grain of wheat, a follower, a servant —these are all terms used by Jesus to describe his radical teaching on what it means to truly know him. But much of his teaching is misinterpreted, misunderstood and misapplied. Many evangelical teachers today view discipleship as a process of sanctification or as a second, deeper commitment, not having anything to do with the conditions for entering the kingdom of God.

The word disciple is the Greek word *mathetes,* which means a learner. However, this definition is inadequate when used in relationship with Jesus Christ for he amplifies the term far beyond its basic Greek meaning. Just as the

37

word for love, as normally used in Greek culture, was expanded and redefined by the writers of the New Testament, so the term disciple is given a whole new depth of meaning by Jesus. The normative meaning of the term in the Jewish and Greek cultures of Jesus' day was that of one who committed himself to a teacher to become a learner. But when scripture uses the term in relation to Jesus Christ it gives an expanded meaning to the term for the obvious reason that we are not merely dealing with a human teacher in Jesus, but with the incarnate God! Our concept of discipleship must be according to *Jesus' definition* and his words must be the standard by which we define the term. It is true that a disciple of Jesus will be a learner. But a disciple of Jesus is more than a learner, he is a *follower* who has denied self, taken up a cross and forsaken all to live for Christ and his kingdom. And according to Jesus, only a disciple is a true Christian.

THE DEMANDS OF DISCIPLESHIP AND THE GOSPEL

How does the discipleship teaching of Jesus fit into the overall scheme of the gospel of grace and salvation? To properly interpret this, we must understand the purpose of creation. We were not only created by God, but created to fulfil a specific purpose. Colossians 1:16 says that all things have been created 'by Him and *for* Him.' We have been created for God. He, himself, is to be the supreme purpose for our existence and the object of our love: 'I am the Lord your God...you shall have no other gods before Me' (Ex. 20:2-3).

This is reiterated by the Lord Jesus when he says that the first and greatest of all the commandments is: 'You shall love the Lord your God with all your heart, and with all your soul, and with all your mind' (Mt. 22:37). God himself is to be the center of our lives. He is to have first place in our affections, the preeminent place in our hearts. No other person or thing must be allowed to displace him from his rightful place in our hearts. And no other purpose should be more important than knowing and doing the will of God. My own personal will, ambitions or interests, or those of another should never to take precedence over the will of God.

Man was created to be under God's authority, to love him supremely, and to live in obedience to his will. Man's fundamental problem, however, is that he does not live this way. He has rebelled against his Creator and does not live to fulfil God's will but his own. The Bible calls this sin. God no longer holds his rightful place in the heart of man. The pursuit of personal happiness and self rule dominates the life rather than God. Men do not live under God's rule but have become authorities unto themselves, living independently of him. Man is alienated and separated from God and is not rightly related to him as a person. Man exists in a *state* of sin and produces specific acts of sin.

THE GOSPEL AND SALVATION

The gospel is a message of reconciliation. It tells us that the just demands of God's law, to which all men are accountable have been fulfilled through the life and death of Christ. But salvation means much more than a declaration of forgiveness, acceptance with God and the assurance that one has been delivered from hell. It means cleansing from guilt and defilement. But it also means restoration. An individual repents of sin and rebellion, and God takes his rightful place in the life. That person now begins to fulfil the purpose for which he was created. He now no longer lives for himself but for Jesus Christ. In other words, salvation is deliverance from sin—its guilt and its power. Repentance is a turning from sin and selfishness with wholehearted commitment to God. This is conversion.

In the passages we have looked at Jesus is defining and

applying the truth of repentance. He tells us what it means in practical terms. The specific things which Jesus mentions in Luke 14—other relationships, one's own life, possessions—are the very things which can displace God from his rightful place of preeminence in the heart. These are idols and Jesus says they must be torn down and cast away. Jonathan Edwards underscores this truth in these words:

> The apostasy of man summarily consists in departing from the true God, to idols; forsaking his Creator and setting up other things in his room...The gods which a natural man worships, instead of the God that made him, are himself and the world...They are not willing to accept Christ; for in doing so, they must of necessity part with all their sins; they must sell the world, and part with their own righteousness...He is a Savior appointed of God; he anointed him, and sent him into the world. And in performing the work of redemption, he wrought the works of God; always did those things that pleased him; and all that he does as a Savior, is to his glory. And one great thing he aimed at in redemption, was to deliver them from their idols, and bring them to God.[22]

Finally Jesus gives the warning in Luke 14:28–32 to count the cost of becoming his disciple. Why? Because he is in this world to build and to battle. He is here to further his kingdom. Any man who comes to him must forsake all (Lk. 14:33), submit his life to Jesus Christ as Lord and follow him to live for his kingdom. This is the nature of repentance. J.I. Packer makes this point in the following comments:

> Repentance is more than just sorrow for the past; repentance is a change of mind and heart, a new life of denying self and serving the Savior as King in self's

place...More than once Christ deliberately called attention to the radical break with the past that *repentance* involves. Luke 9:23,24—'If any man will come after Me, let him deny himself and take up his cross and follow Me, whosoever will lose his life for My sake the same (but only he) will save it'. Luke 14:26,33—'If any man come to Me and hate not his father and mother and wife and children and brethren and sisters yea and his own life also (i.e., put them all decisively second in his esteem) he cannot be my disciple. . .whosoever he be of you that forsaketh not all that he hath, he cannot be My disciple.' The*repentance* that Christ requires of His people consists in a settled refusal to set any limit to the claims which He may make on their lives.[23]

Christ's call to discipleship is in principle the same call of God given to lost men and women during the Old Testament days of Ezekiel. It is a call to repentance—a turning from and forsaking of idolatry and sin:

Then some of the elders of Israel came to me and sat down before me. And the word of the Lord came to me saying, 'Son of man, these men have set up their idols in their hearts, and have put right before their faces the stumbling block of their iniquity. Should I be consulted by them at all? Therefore speak to them and tell them, Thus says the Lord God, Any man of the house of Israel who sets up his idols in his heart, puts right before his face the stumbling block of his iniquity, and then comes to the prophet, I the Lord will be brought to give him an answer in the matter in view of the multitude of his idols, in order to lay hold of the hearts of the house of Israel who are estranged from Me through all their idols.

Therefore say to the house of Israel, Thus says the Lord God, Repent and turn away from your idols, and turn your faces away from all your abominations.'

Therefore I will judge you, O house of Israel, each according to his conduct declares the Lord God. Repent and turn away from all your transgressions, so that iniquity may not become a stumbling block to you. Cast away from you all your transgressions which you have committed, and make yourselves a new heart and a new spirit! For why will you die, O house of Israel? For I have no pleasure in the death of anyone who dies, declares the Lord God. Therefore, repent and live (Ez. 14:1-6, 18:30-32).

This word of the prophet is echoed in the New Testament by Jesus when he says, 'Unless you repent, you will all likewise perish' (Lk. 13:3). Jesus is saying is that to become a Christian, one must become a disciple. The two are synonymous terms. The Bible knows of no such concept as that taught so widely today that a person can be a Christian and yet not be a disciple. The Lord Jesus forever nullifies such a concept by his teaching. If a man does not become a disciple by denying self and enthroning Jesus as Lord, he will perish. Acts 11:26 tells us that 'the disciples were called Christians first in Antioch.' Before they ever received the name Christian they were called disciples.

Therefore to sum up, we see that the essence of sin is self–will and self–rule. In other words living for self. Sin is defined in 1 John 3:4 where we are told 'sin is lawlessness.' Vines *Expository Dictionary* says that lawlessness is 'the displacement of the will of God with the will of self.' Therefore sin in its essence is self–will. Or as John Stott puts it, 'sin is self.' Repentance means turning from sin. Dr. Thiessen says, 'In conversion faith is the turning of the soul to God as repentance *is the turning of the* soul *from sin.*'[24]

Therefore since the essence of sin is self–will, repentance is turning from self–will or self–rule and submitting the life to Jesus as Lord, thereby becoming his disciple. If a man has not dethroned self and enthroned Jesus as Lord, he is still living in self–will and self–rule and has therefore not truly repented. He will perish. Repentance is towards God. It is a change of mind toward God as the rightful ruler and authority in one's life. The scriptures emphasize salvation as a total concept. Justification is but one aspect of salvation. Salvation is in Jesus Christ. *He* is the Savior. *He* has done the work. It is by his merits and his alone that any individual is forgiven and accepted by God. His righteousness is imputed to the believer. Salvation becomes the personal possession of an individual when Christ becomes the personal possession of the individual and he is in turn possessed by Christ. Salvation is applied to an individual through union with Christ. Salvation comes by receiving Christ as prophet, priest and king through repentance and faith. I trust him as Savior and commit myself to him as Lord. The Westminster Confession says:

> The principal acts of saving faith are, accepting, receiving, and resting upon Christ alone for justification, sanctification, and eternal life, by virtue of the covenant of grace (XIV.2).[25]

The Confession states that saving faith involves receiving Christ for justification and also for sanctification. What it means to receive Christ for sanctification is described by the Puritan theologian John Owen in these words:

> Obedience unto Christ does not consist merely in doing the things which He requireth...All obedience unto Christ proceeds from an express subjection of our souls and consciences unto Him.[26]

What Owen is saying is that the *process* of sanctification will begin when there is first a *commitment* characterized by submission to Christ. The process flows out of the commitment. John Murray points out that the term sanctification in scripture has two meanings: an initial

43

commitment and consecration of the life to Christ from the world and sin, which he calls 'definitive sanctification', and the process of growth in the Christian life. He describes it in these terms:

When we speak of sanctification we generally think of it as a process by which the believer is gradually transformed in heart, mind, will, and conduct, and conformed more and more to the will of God and to the image of Christ, until at death the disembodied spirit is made perfect in holiness, and at the resurrection his body likewise will be conformed to the likeness of the body of Christ's glory. It is biblical to apply the term 'sanctification' to this process of transformation and conformation. But it is a fact too frequently overlooked that in the New Testament the most characteristic terms that refer to sanctification are used, not of a process, but of a once–for–all definitive act. We properly think of calling, regeneration, justification, and adoption as acts of God effected once for all, and not requiring or admitting of repetition. It is of their nature to be definitive. But a considerable part of the New Testament teaching places sanctification in this category. We are... compelled to take account of the fact that the language of sanctification is used with reference to some decisive action that occurs at the inception of the Christian life, and one that characterizes the people of God in their identity as called effectually by God's grace. It would be, therefore, a deflection from biblical patterns of language and conception to think of sanctification exclusively in terms of a progressive work...What is this sanctification?...The person who lives in sin, or to sin, lives and acts in the realm of sin—it is the sphere of his life and activity. And the person who died to sin no longer lives in that sphere. His tie with it has been broken, and he has been translated into another realm...*This is the decisive cleavage that the apostle has in view; it is the foundation upon*

44

which rests his whole conception of a believer's life, and it is
a cleavage, a breach, a translation as really and decisively
true in the sphere of moral and religious relationship as in
ordinary experience of death. *There is a once–for–all
definitive and irreversible breach with the realm in which sin
reigns in and unto death...This means that there is a decisive
and definitive breach with the power and service of sin in the
case of every one who has come under the control of the
provisions of grace* (emphasis mine).[27]

A saved man is a man who has received Christ as Savior *and*
Lord. He is both justified and sanctified. He is regenerated
and converted. Because of union with Christ and a new
nature, he lives a life in conformity to Jesus Christ in the
power of his resurrection by the enabling of the indwelling
Spirit. Where there is no submission to Christ as Lord there
simply is no true Christianity. James Montgomery Boice
offers this sober warning regarding the salvation teachings
of the Lord Jesus Christ:

There is a fatal defect in the life of Christ's church in the
twentieth century: a lack of true discipleship. Discipleship
means forsaking everything to follow Christ. But for many
of today's supposed Christians—perhaps the majority—it
is the case that while there is much talk about Christ and
even much furious activity, there is actually very little
following of Christ Himself. And that means in some
circles there is very little genuine Christianity. Many who
fervently call Him 'Lord, Lord' are not Christians
(Matthew 7:21)...There are several reasons that the
situation I have described is common in today's church.
The first is a defective theology that has crept over us like
a deadening fog. This theology separates faith from
discipleship and grace from obedience. It teaches that
Jesus can be received as one's Savior without being
received as one's Lord...Discipleship in not a supposed

second step in Christianity, as if one first became a believer in Jesus and then, if he chooses, a disciple. From the beginning, discipleship is involved in what it means to be a Christian....Is 'faith' minus commitment a true biblical faith?...If faith without works is dead—how much truer is it that faith without commitment is dead...True faith involves these elements: knowledge...heart response...and commitment, without which 'faith' is no different from the assent of the demons who 'believe...and shudder' (James 2:19). [28]

A.W. Tozer makes these comments:

The sinner is actually a rebel against properly constituted authority. That is what makes sin—sin. We are rebels. We are sons of disobedience. Sin is the breaking of the law and we are in rebellion and we are fugitives *from* the just laws of God while we are sinners. The root of sin is rebellion against law, rebellion against God. Does not the sinner say, I belong to myself. I owe allegiance to no one unless I choose to give it. That is the essence of sin. Thus in repentance, we reverse that relationship and we fully submit to the Word of God and the will of God as obedient children. We have no basis to believe that we can come casually and sprightly to the Lord Jesus and say, I have come for some help, Lord Jesus. I understand that you are the Savior so I am going to believe and be saved and then I am going to turn away and think about the other matters of lordship and allegiance and obedience at some other time in the future.

I warn you, you will not get help from Him in that way for the Lord will not save those whom He cannot command. He will not divide His offices. You cannot believe on a half Christ. We take Him for what He is, the anointed Savior and Lord who is King of Kings and Lord of Lords.[29]

The Bible makes it very clear that submission to the Lordship of Christ is a necessary condition for salvation. This is seen not only in Mark 8:34-37 but also is clearly stated or implied in the following verses:

> For to this end Christ died and lived again, that He might be Lord both of the dead and of the living (Rom. 14:9).

> That if you confess with your mouth Jesus as Lord, and shalt believe in your heart that God raised Him from the dead, you shall be saved (Rom. 10:9).

> But now having been freed from sin and enslaved to God you derive your benefit, resulting in sanctification, and the outcome, eternal life (Rom. 6:22).

> He died for all, that they who live should no longer live for themselves, but for Him who died and rose again on their behalf (2 Cor. 5:15).

> For they themselves report about us what kind of reception we had with you, and how you turned to God from idols to serve a living and true God (I Thes. 1:9)

THE ISSUE OF WORKS

The Bible clearly teaches that salvation is a gift of God and not of works lest any man should boast (Ephesians 2:8,9). Conservative evangelicals emphasize and rightly so, that no man can work his way to heaven. They preach consistently and forcefully against good works as a basis for salvation. They preach the need of turning by faith to Christ alone as the Savior, resting in his finished work and in the merits of his shed blood and righteousness. We commonly hear, 'Baptism will not save you, church membership will not save you, tithing, witnessing, your moral life, your good deeds, your fastings, your prayers, indulgences, etc. None of these things can give you a standing before God.'

There must indeed be a turning from all self–righteousness if one is to come to know Jesus Christ as Savior. However, many of the same evangelicals who preach the need to turn from self–righteousness in order to be saved will not preach repentance from self–will and self–rule. Why? Many wrongly believe that demanding men to turn from self–will adds works to the gospel of grace. The question is this: What is the difference between turning from self–righteousness to Jesus as Savior and self–will to Jesus as Lord? If the one is a form of works then so is the other.

The fact is, neither of them is works. Repentant, saving faith is a gift from God. Faith is a gift from God (Eph 2:8) as is repentance (Acts 11: 18): 'When they heard these things, they held their peace and glorified God saying, Then hath God also to the Gentiles granted repentance unto life.'

Jesus Christ is both Savior and Lord. He cannot be divided. If a man comes to Jesus he comes to him as he is, as both Lord and Savior. There must be a turning from self–righteousness for Jesus to be Savior and there must be a turning from self–will or self–rule for Jesus to be Lord. This is not a form of works but true biblical repentance which is a gift from God. True repentance is turning *from* self, while faith is turning *to* Christ. The result is conversion.

As A.W. Pink says, 'Repentance is the negative side of conversion. Conversion is a whole hearted turning unto God, but there cannot be a turning unto without a turning from. Sin must be forsaken ere one can draw nigh unto the Holy One. As it is written, "Ye turned to God from idols to serve (live for) the living and true God" (I Thessalonians 1:9).'[30]

We need to distinguish between discipleship as an initial commitment and discipleship as a process, for it is both. Much of the confusion about commitment to Christ as

Lord as 'works salvation' comes from a failure to distinguish between the two. When Christ calls men to himself he calls them to a *commitment* of discipleship, as we have seen. From that commitment issues a life of good works in discipleship or sanctification. But unless this initial commitment is made there will be no new life of holiness because there is no union with Christ. The Holy Spirit does not indwell the heart. The individual is not converted. Many do not make the biblical distinction between an initial lordship or discipleship *commitment* and the *process* of sanctification. If we understand the distinction between the *commitment* of discipleship and the *process* of discipleship which is growth in sanctification, the confusion can be avoided.

THE RESULTS OF REPENTANT FAITH

What will be the result in the life of a person who truly repents and believes? The result will be a totally changed life. The overall bent or direction of the life, from the heart attitudes and motivations to the outward behavior, completely changes. Where the life used to be centered around self and the pursuit of selfish interests, it is now centered around Christ and His interests.

No Christian will live a perfect life, but the desire of the heart—the practice or habit of the new creature in Christ—is to know and do the will of God. The issue is not perfection, but a changed life. If a person's life has not been fundamentally changed from one of self centeredness to one of living for the will of God, then that person has never come to know Jesus Christ. The evidence of true conversion is a changed life.

This is clearly taught in the Bible. Matthew 7:21 and I John 2:17 emphatically state that the only people who will enter the kingdom of heaven, possess eternal life and abide forever are those who *do* the will of God.

Not everyone who says to Me, 'Lord, Lord,' will enter the kingdom of heaven; but he who does the will of My Father who is in heaven (Mt. 7:21).

Do not love the world, nor the things in the world. If any one loves the world, the love of the Father is not in him...And the world is passing away, and also its lusts; but the one who does the will of God abides for ever (I Jn. 2:15,17).

In I John 2:1 we read, 'My little children, I am writing these things to you that you may not sin. And if anyone sins, we have an Advocate with the Father, Jesus Christ the righteous.'

I John 1:9 it says, 'If we confess our sins, He is faithful and righteous to forgive us our sins and to cleanse us from all unrighteousness.'

The apostle John readily admits in these verses that the possibility of sin is very real. He does not teach perfection but in the book of 1 John he teaches that if a person's life is not characterized by change, that person has never come to know Jesus Christ. In other words he has never truly repented and believed.

He says in I John 5:13 that he has written what he has written in order that men might know if they really possess eternal life. He says if a person has really believed in the Son he has life: 'He who has the Son has life' (I Jn. 5:12). But how does one know whether or not he has the Son and therefore has life? The answer to that question is clear. If the life passes the tests he has written about in all that precedes chapter five, the person can know he has eternal life. If the things he writes about are not evidenced in the life, then that person does not have the Son and therefore he does not have life. He has not believed savingly. He has what James calls 'dead faith' because he has no works or changed life.

John is not teaching perfection. Again, the issue is not perfection; the issue is a changed life. The following are some of the tests he gives:

> And by this we know that we have come to know Him, if we keep His commandments. The one who says, 'I have come to know Him,' and does not keep His commandments, is a liar, and the truth is not in him (I Jn . 2:3,4).

> Do not love the world, nor the things in the world. If any one loves the world, the love of the Father is not in him. For all that is in the world, the lust of the flesh and the lust of the eyes and the boastful pride of life, is not from the Father, but is from the world. And the world is passing away, and also its lusts; but the one who does the will of God abides for ever (I Jn. 2:15–17).

> No one who is born of God practices sin; because His seed abides in him: and he cannot sin, because he is born of God. By this the children of God and the children of the devil are obvious: anyone who does not practice righteousness is not of God, nor the one who does not love his brother (I Jn. 3:9,10).

> We know that we have passed out of death into life, because we love the brethren (I Jn. 3:14).

J.C. Ryle states:

> To be 'born of God' is to be the subject of an inward change of heart, so complete, that it is like passing into a new existence. It is the introduction into the human soul of a seed from heaven, a new principle, a Divine nature, a new will. Certainly it is no outward bodily alteration; but it is no less certain that it is an entire alteration of the inward man. It adds no new faculties to our minds; but it gives an

entirely new bent and bias to our old ones. The tastes and opinions of one 'born again,' his views of sin, of the world, of the Bible, of God, and of Christ, are so thoroughly new, that he is to all intents and purposes what St. Paul calls la new creature. In fact, as the Church Catechism truly says, it is 'a death unto sin and a new birth unto righteousness.'[31]

John MacArthur makes the following comments about the necessity for a changed life:

The church again is facing an age–old problem—the invasion of it by what has become known as 'easy believism' or 'cheap grace'... People are told just to 'believe in Jesus' and everything will be settled forever...Our Lord recognized the potential problem of an easy believism, as indicated in John 8:30,31, 'As He spoke these things, many came to believe in Him. Jesus therefore was saying to those Jews who had believed in Him, "If you abide in My word, then you are truly disciples of Mine".' Jesus affirms that an easy believism is inadequate.

The concept of easy believism is contrary also to the message of the New Testament epistles regarding salvation and assurance. The life of a true believer is never portrayed as a soft, do–as–you–please existence. The believer is called to a life of obedience, in which faith is verified by conduct. A life of obedience should flow from a Christian's basic relationship to Christ. The Beatitudes call for a full self–examination. Such an approach Paul calls for in 2 Corinthians 13:5, 'Test yourselves to see if you are in the faith.' Prove it, he's saying. If it were easy to point to an experience in the past to prove your salvation, why would Paul ask you to examine yourself? There must be something else here.

You might be saying, 'Well, I'm a Christian. I believe. I made a decision for Christ.' A lot of people point to the past to verify their salvation, but did you know that the

Bible never does that? It never points to the past. It always
bases proof of real salvation on your life now. *Examine
(test* in NASB) is a present tense continuous action, 'Be
constantly examining yourselves'...Righteousness is the
issue. Righteousness sets us apart as converted.
Righteousness simply means living right, living under
God's standards, by His definition—If we do not live this
way, the genuineness of our salvation is open to
suspicion—to others and to ourselves (usually in the form
of insecurity). Hebrews 12:14 haunts me when I meet
people who claim to be Christians but whose lives do not
agree: 'Sanctification without which no one will see the
Lord.' Second Timothy 2:19 says that the Lord knows them
that are His. And who are they? Those that name the
name of Christ and depart from iniquity. Titus 1: 16 says,
'They profess to know God, but by their deeds they deny
Him, being detestable and disobedient, and worthless for
any good deeds.' Profession means nothing without
obedience, without righteousness, without holiness,
without departing from iniquity. Once, I actually heard a
pastor preach, 'Isn't it wonderful that you can come to
Jesus Christ and you don't have to change anything on the
inside or the outside?' Can that be true? Of course not.
There had better be transformation. Of course we can
come to Jesus just as we are, but if we come away from
conversion just as we were, how can we call it conversion?
Second Corinthians 5:17 sums it up well: 'Therefore if any
man be in Christ, he is a new creature; the old things passed
away; behold, new things have come.'

Being righteous does not mean that we never sin. First
John 1:9 says Christians are constantly confessing their sin.
That certainly indicates that we do sin. But it is sin that we
deal with sooner or later. We confess it, we turn from it, we
repent of it, we despise it. We do not love it. 'If anyone
loves the world, the love of the Father is not in him' (I John
2:15)...You cannot prove that you are a Christian by

waltzing down the same old path. Having made a decision, having walked an aisle, having gone into an inquiry room, or having read through a little book was never the biblical criterion for salvation. The biblical criterion for salvation is what Your life is like right now...In Matthew 5:13 Christ calls us the salt of the earth and in verse 14, the light of the world. If you are really a Christian, your testimony will be clearly, decisively distinguishable from the rest of the world.

Don't claim to be a Christian because five years ago you walked an aisle. Don't claim to be a Christian because you once signed a card. Don't try to tell God you're a Christian because you went into a prayer room and talked to a counselor. And don't even tell yourself you're a Christian because some counselor told you that you were, because, at that moment, he didn't know positively, either.

Assurance is the Holy Spirit's work. He grants it by the *inward* testimony (Romans 8) and by the outer exhibit of works. Faith without works is dead, James says. Jesus puts it this way in John 8:31, 'If you abide in My word, then You are truly disciples of Mine.' He is saying you will be characterized by right thinking, obedience, right talking and right doing...Don't lull yourself to sleep. Beloved, examine yourselves whether you are in the faith. Prove yourselves...If you have not committed your life to Christ and come into the kingdom on His terms, you had better do it while you can.[32]

When did *your* life change? When did you turn from living for yourself and surrender yourself unreservedly to Jesus as Lord to become his disciple? When did you come to him on his terms as he has defined it in Mark 8, John 12, Luke 14 and Matthew 11? *Who* do you live for, yourself or Jesus Christ? Who rules your life? *What* do you live for? This world and the fulfillment of your own interests, plans and ambitions or the kingdom of God?

When did you deny self and take up a cross and die to yourself that you might follow Jesus Christ to be what He wants you to be, to go where He would have you go, to do what He would have you do?

When did you forsake all to follow him? In other words, when did you repent? 'Unless you repent, you will ... perish' (Lk. 13:3).

Conclusion

In light of the teaching of Jesus and the word of God it is clear that a part of the Church in this day has drifted away from the gospel which the Lord Jesus commanded to be preached to all the world and which the the scriptures so clearly define for us.

There is a great deception today in our evangelical world which is leading multitudes to damnation. This deception comes in a gospel preached which assures a man of salvation without repentance, possession of Jesus as Savior without submission to him as Lord, and an optional discipleship. This is a false gospel.

The word of God, the Lord Jesus Christ and great conservative evangelical theologians of the past and present have all consistently taught this truth: No man can become a Christian who does not repent of sin. And that means the dethroning of self and the submission of one's life to Jesus as Lord.

Yet the common teaching of our day is that a person need 'only believe' in Jesus or simply to 'receive' Jesus as one's own personal Savior in order to be saved. There is virtually nothing said about repentance. If the word is mentioned at all, it is rarely, if ever, defined. And when repentance is preached it is generally with reference to sinful behavior only. We rarely hear of the need for personal submission to the Lordship of Jesus Christ. Yet the Lord Jesus himself makes it abundantly clear that this is necessary for salvation and the essence of true repentance.

We live in a day when the conditions for salvation need to

be clearly defined. We need to come back to the first principles of the word of God. We need to teach and preach what the word of God says, faithfully and uncompromisingly. We cannot afford to be wrong about the gospel, for ourselves or in our teaching. The issue at stake is eternity.

The modern gospel of 'easy–believism' is not truth, it is half truth. It is a masterpiece of deception. It strips the gospel of its commitment and leaves the sinner in his rebellion and sin, while professing the name of Jesus Christ. The Amplified Bible says that the nature of the antichrist is to come 'to oppose Christ in the guise of Christ' (I Jn. 2:18). This is precisely what today's 'easy-believism' gospel does. By omitting the call for true repentance and by appealing to men to 'only believe' or simply to accept Jesus as their Savior only, this incomplete gospel is being offered to men in the name of Jesus but leaves them in a condition of rebellion, and therefore of opposition to him. For if a man does not yield to Jesus as Lord, he stands opposed to him.

R. C. H. Lenski says 'the greatest and most fatal work of lawlessness is to pervert the Lord's Word in the Lord's own name and to foist this perversion upon others.' [33] This is precisely what the gospel of 'easy–believism' does. It perverts the Lord's word in the Lord's own name and this perversion is then foisted upon others.

It is both necessary and right that we emphasize the fact that Jesus Christ is Savior and that he alone can deal with our sins and that no amount of good works can make us acceptable to God and that there must be a turning from self–righteousness to Jesus as Savior.

However, a gospel message that emphasizes the Saviorhood of Christ to the exclusion of his Lordship, failing to present to men the necessity of also turning from self–will to Jesus as Lord, is a gospel message that deceives men. The Bible says a man must repent and believe, not just believe. Faith without repentance is dead faith. That kind of faith may profess Jesus Christ, but it does not result in a changed life.

As one looks at the state of the Church in the day in which we live, most would agree that its general state is appalling. It is characterized by worldliness, prayerlessness, materialism and an overall lack of reality. Many decry this state of affairs but seem at a loss to know what the answer is.

The Church needs to return to the first principles of the gospel. When those who are responsible for teaching and preaching the word of God return to the *whole* gospel then the Spirit of God will witness to that message with power because it is a message which glorifies Jesus Christ.

The only answer and hope for the Church, our culture and world in which we are living is a moving of the Spirit of God. But he is only going to own and witness to that message which is consistent with the truth of scripture and which glorifies the Lord Jesus Christ.

A message which omits the summons for men to submit their lives to Jesus as Lord is inconsistent with the truth of God's word. It does not glorify the Lord Jesus and therefore the Spirit does not move in power to bring men into the kingdom of God. The result is that you have multitudes of people in evangelical churches who have responded to only half the gospel and consequently their hearts have never been changed.

I plead with you to examine your own heart before the Lord to make absolutely certain you have truly repented and that you are in the kingdom of God. And if you teach or preach the word of God I implore you to search the scriptures and examine the gospel you present to men in the light of what the Word of God teaches. It is a terrible responsibility to teach the scriptures. Are you teaching men the whole truth so that you can stand before your Lord and God with clean hands?

Let me close with these words by A.W. Tozer: 'Search the Scriptures, read the New Testament and if you see that I have given a germ of truth, then I urge you to do something about it. If you have been led to believe imperfectly in a divided Saviour be glad there is still time for you to do something about it.'[34]

And I would add, if you have been led to preach or teach half truth concerning the Lord Jesus Christ and the gospel, be glad there is still time for you to do something about it.

Personal Testimony

We have looked at the word of God, the teaching of Jesus and the writings of godly men, but the practical application of these truths was brought home very forcefully to me by the experience of my wife Paula. The following is her testimony in her own words.

If you had asked me a few years ago if I was a Christian, I would have responded with an immediate and very emphatic, YES! The question would have surprised me as I had never doubted my salvation. It would never have occurred to me to do so. Having been brought up in a Christian home, I had professed faith in Jesus as a child, and had accepted without question the Bible as the inerrant word of God. I believed, therefore I was a Christian.

Though unhappy and rebellious as a teen, I settled down in my twenties to a normal life of marriage and children. I rededicated my life to God and determined to make up for lost time and wasted opportunity. To that end, I applied myself earnestly and diligently. It was my desire to really know God and please Him, so I purposed to achieve this goal beginning with a daily quiet time and prayer. I memorized scripture, read 'how to' books, attended Bible studies and conferences and even went witnessing.

Years passed and my activity increased. I was a teacher, a leader, a discipler of others. I was doing all the right things and from all appearances, I was doing well. But I knew that in reality I was getting nowhere. It was all mechanical. The deep need and desire of my heart was not being met, and I was no closer to achieving my goal. I felt the frustrated unhappiness and rebellion of my teens beginning to return. Life was still empty and meaningless in spite of all my effort. For all my striving to know God, He was still a distant and impersonal Being of Whom I was much afraid and before Whom I felt continually unclean and unsure. I was growing in my knowledge of facts relating to Jesus, but not growing closer to Him. And although those facts had altered my behavior, checking sin externally to a degree, they hadn't changed my heart. Every effort to claim verses, to appropriate Christ, or to pray through to victory ended in total failure. I was being conformed to a system of Biblical principles, but not into the image of Jesus Christ. For all my learning and activity, two things were still missing in my life: personal (instead of mere factual) knowledge of Jesus Christ and the capacity to live a holy, obedient life **within.**

As I studied the Bible, desperately hoping to find an answer to my problem, I was confronted with, confounded by, and attracted to the lives of two men: David in the Old Testament and Paul in the New. What confounded yet attracted me was the relationship each had with their God. It was with both, a thing of the heart first and foremost. Then, as a result, their lives were conformed to the will of God expressed in His word. It was cause and effect. The cause? Love. The effect? Obedience from a heart of love. I, however, was trying to produce a heart for God by being obedient. My obedience was external at best in spite of my most valiant efforts. Consequently, I knew that I was no closer to knowing and loving God than I'd ever been.

The relationship that David and Paul enjoyed with the Lord made me both envious and angry. I wanted it too, but couldn't figure out how to get it. They not only knew about God, they knew God. They delighted in Him, communed with Him, heard from Him, were comforted, encouraged, strengthened, protected, provided for, and led by Him. They knew not just the Word of God, but the God of the

Word. They were men right with God, loved of God and they knew it; not as fact only, but as an experience. The object of their devotion and faith was a Person, God's Word being a means to an end, pointing them to Himself, not an end in itself.

As a young girl I'd been programmed like every other little girl I knew to believe that getting married, having children and a nice home would mean security, happiness and fulfillment. I had it all now, but was not secure, happy or fulfilled. Instead, I was miserable. Maybe, I reasoned, being a wife and mother worked out better for others like Christianity worked out better for people like David and Paul. But as for me, I was as big a failure as a wife and mother as I was as a 'Christian.' I was thoroughly disillusioned and disappointed not only with myself but with my circumstances as well. However, I felt as duty bound to try to be a good wife and mother as I felt duty bound to try to be a good Christian. But I carried out my obligations to my family as I carried them out to God; it was service without heart. I resented my responsibilities and the restrictions placed upon me. There was no compensation or enjoyment in all my serving, Godward or manward. And there was no way out. I couldn't leave, and I couldn't seem to find a way to cope. So I made a way of escape for myself. I retreated mentally to a dream world of *if onlys*, where I imagined myself in other relationships and circumstances more pleasant and satisfying. I entertained myself with little homemade mental movies in which I starred as what I wasn't; secure, happy, fulfilled—a success instead of a failure. In these little dreams I lived out my desires and ambitions. I achieved my goals. I had my way. The little dreams were all I had to keep me from going under in despair as I had to face my real daily life, knowing that I was powerless to change either myself or my circumstances. Surely there must be an answer. I pursued and exhausted every possible option. I read and prayed and sought counsel from pastors and friends. What was wrong with me? And why could I not lay hold of the Lord or experience His victory and power in my life over sin and selfishness? I did everything I'd read that I must do, and everything that I'd been told to do to conquer the sin within but managed only a kind of reformation but no transformation. I was like a wild horse. I'd been corralled, but in my nature, I was still a wild horse. My circumstances were like a fence that held me in. The problem was not my circumstances and I knew it. The problem was me. I needed to be changed. I needed not a change in my situation, but a changed attitude and outlook. I became more and more convinced that my help must come from God, not man. And I began to look away from other resources to Him, praying with a greater sense of urgency as my need deepened. Lord, I prayed, whatever is wrong with my heart, make it right. Change me.

By September 10, 1981, I reached a crisis point. As I prayed continually and desperately for divine intervention, it seemed as though the enemy sought to destroy me with depression before the answer could come. Sin and selfishness dominated my life and the harder I tried to deal with them, the more powerful a hold they had on me. I seemed carried along by something I couldn't control. I was controlled by a self life I hated but had no authority over or power to deny. Sin reigned. In spite of my professed faith in Christ, I could not 'do all things through him who strengthens me.' I was very near the breaking point.

In the quiet of that afternoon, as I tried once more to think my way through to an answer, a verse came to mind. Matthew 16:25, 'For whosoever will save his life shall lose it, and whosoever will lose his life for my sake shall find it.'

In that instant, I saw the answer. I must 'lose' my life. I'd been seeking to find my life. As a child, I sought the admiration and praise of others to give me a sense of personal identity and worth through accomplishments:

academic and musical. As an adult, I sought happiness and fulfillment for myself in relationships and the acquisition of possessions for security and respectability. My life was occupied totally with me; my desire to be happy, what to pursue or obtain to make me happy, resenting anyone or anything that was an obstacle to my goal. But seek as I had, for true happiness and satisfaction, they eluded me. When the object or person pursued became mine, disappointment and dissatisfaction were all that I experienced.

So I saw in that moment, that to find life, I must lose my life, turn my back on it, die to it, give it up to God. I must give Him my life with all its secret desires, ambitions, expectations, disappointments and needs. I must turn not only from sins, but from myself, the sum total of me and all that I'd ever wanted for myself in this world. I must give myself without reserve to God, my past, present and future. The issue was not merely behavior control, but control of my whole being. He must control and my part was to submit absolutely, yield entirely, follow without hesitation. It was a decision to become a sheep. To get a new heart then, the old one had to go. I must give it to God.

For a moment, I struggled. It wasn't an easy thing to die and I was afraid. Would there really be anything truly satisfying on the other side? Was this really the answer? Did I really have to surrender everything, to die?

I had to find out. I lifted my hands and said quietly, 'You win lord. I'm giving you all.'

I'm reluctant to share the experience which followed because experiences differ with different people, but conversion *is* an experience and I know now that it would be impossible for anyone to be truly converted without experiencing some change.

At the moment I surrendered my life entirely to God, I knew that He had heard me and had accepted my surrender. I was conscious immediately, that a great burden had been rolled away. I knew that I'd been forgiven

65

and cleansed. I knew that I had been changed. Peace, like a great calm following a storm at sea and joy unspeakable filled my heart. I knew that the great war within had ceased. The sense that all had been made right replaced the agitation and restlessness I had felt only minutes before. I had finally been subdued and conquered by the Lord of Glory before Whom I now gladly and gratefully bowed. And He no longer seemed distant or impersonal nor I unclean, and unsure before Him.

The change in my life was so revolutionary that in the days following my surrender I felt I must understand exactly what had happened to me. As I prayed, another verse came to mind. 2 Corinthians 5:17 – 'Therefore if any man be in Christ, he is a new creature: old things are passed away, behold all things are become new.' I was certainly a new creature and astounded at the transformation. It was clearly a work done in me, and not one I could have worked up myself. My outlook and attitude, Godward and manward, was totally and miraculously changed. There was a very real love in my heart towards God and for His Word and a keen desire to show my gratitude to Him by living an obedient and holy life if He would only show me how. I could say with Saul when he 'fell to the earth' before Jesus at his conversion, **'Lord,** what wilt thou have me to do?' (Acts 9:4,6). 1 had become a new creature. The old things had passed away as a dark cloud and all things were new!

It was very clear. I'd just been born again, saved. But what of my earlier profession of faith in Jesus? It had been a dead faith, an intellectual acceptance of facts relating to Jesus. But those facts had never affected my life. I'd committed myself to facts, to truth but not to the Person those facts were about. And I had acknowledged my sinfulness, trying to turn from acts of sin without ever turning from the cause of sin – me.

The evidence of true conversion is salvation, Jesus came

to save sinners. From what? From themselves, from sin (its power and dominion—see Romans 6) and Satan. It is ludicrous to think that Jesus would save us from hell only, but not insist on saving us from ourselves, changing us to fit us for heaven. In fact, how could He save us from hell without saving us from that which will send us there? We are sinners, and the essence or root of our sin is our willful rebellion against or refusal to come under the sovereign authority and control of God. By 'accepting Him as Savior' and 'making Him Lord' sometime later, the wretched 'I' is still in control—cloaked in religion, even doctrinally sound evangelical religion—but only religion—not the robe of righteousness—true Christianity. Hell was created for the devil and his host but will also be the inevitable destination of all those who cry with him, 'We will not have this man to reign over us' (Luke 19:14). The issue is not my profession but who is in possession of my life.

In light of this, what about your profession? Who's in possession of your life? Is your assurance of salvation based on your decision for Him, or *His* work of salvation in you evidenced by changes; the old things have passed away and all things have become new. Are you a new creature in Christ?

Appendix

While we have seen that lordship salvation is the clear teaching of the scriptures and the Lord Jesus Christ, there are those who charge that this teaching is a departure from the reformation and undermines the historic teaching of Protestantism on the nature of saving faith. But such an assertion is simply contrary to truth. Lordship salvation is the doctrine that is consistent with historic reformational teaching and it is the opposite view which is in fact contrary to it and which undermines the meaning of saving faith. This is seen from the following documentation of the teaching of leading evangelical theologians from the past and present on the meaning of repentance and faith.

A.W. Tozer

The scriptures do not teach that the Person of Jesus Christ nor any of the important offices which God has given Him can be divided or ignored according to the whims of men. Therefore I must be frank in my feeling that a notable heresy has come into being throughout our evangelical Christian circles—the widely accepted concept that we humans can choose to accept Christ only because we need Him as Savior and that we have the right to postpone our obedience to Him as Lord as long as we want to!

I think the following is a fair statement of what I was taught in my early Christian experience and it certainly needs a lot of modifying and a great many qualifiers to save us from error:

We are saved by accepting Christ as Savior.

We are sanctified by accepting Christ as Lord.

We may do the first without doing the second.

This concept has sprung up naturally from a misunderstanding of what the Bible actually says about Christian discipleship and obedience.

The truth is that salvation apart from obedience is unknown in the sacred scriptures. Peter makes it plain that we are 'elect according to the foreknowledge of God the Father, through sanctification of the Spirit unto obedience.'

To urge men and women to believe in a divided Christ is bad teaching for no one can receive half of Christ or a third of Christ or a quarter of the Person of Christ!

But how can we insist and teach that our Lord Jesus Christ can be our Savior without being our Lord? How can we continue to teach that we can be saved without any thought of obedience to our Sovereign Lord?

The Bible never in any way gives us any such a concept of salvation. **Nowhere are we ever led to believe that we can use Jesus as Savior and not own Him as our Lord.** He is the Lord and as the Lord He saves us because He has all the offices of Savior and Christ and High Priest and Wisdom and Righteousness and Sanctification and Redemption! He is all of these things and all of these things are embodied in Him as Christ the Lord...**It is either all of Christ or none of Christ.** I believe we need to preach again a whole Christ to the world, a Christ who does not need our apologies, a Christ who will not be divided, **a Christ who will either be Lord of all or who will not be Lord at all**.

In our time we have over emphasized the psychology of the sinner's condition, We spend much time describing the woe of the sinner, the grief of the sinner, and the great burden he carries. He does have all these, but we have overemphasized them until we forget the principal fact, that the sinner is actually a rebel against properly constituted authority. That is what makes sin – sin. We are rebels. We are sons of disobedience. Sin is the breaking of the law and we are in rebellion and we are fugitives from the just laws of God while we are sinners...**the root of sin is rebellion against law, rebellion against God. Does not the sinner say, I belong to myself. I owe allegiance to no one unless I choose to give it. That is the essence of sin. Thus, in repentance, we reverse that relationship and we fully submit to the Word of God and the will of God as obedient children**...We have no basis to believe that we can come casually and sprightly to the Lord Jesus and say, 'I have come for some help, Lord Jesus. I understand that you are the Savior so I am going to believe and be saved and then I am going to turn away and think about the other matters of lordship and allegiance and obedience at some other time in the future.'

I warn you, you will not get help from Him in that way for the Lord will not save those whom He cannot command! He will not divide His offices. You cannot believe on a half Christ. We take Him for what He is, the anointed Savior and Lord who is King of Kings and Lord of all Lords. He would not be who He is if He saved us and called us and chose us without the understanding that He can also guide and control our lives.

Just remember what the Bible says about the Person and the titles and the offices of Jesus. 'God hath made this same Jesus whom ye have crucified both Lord and Christ.' Jesus means Savior, Lord means Sovereign, and Christ means Anointed One. The Apostle therefore did not preach Jesus as Savior. He preached to them Jesus as Lord and Christ and Savior, never dividing His Person or offices. Remember too, that Paul wrote to the Roman Christians, 'What saith it? The word is nigh thee, even in thy mouth and in thy heart, that is the word of faith which we preach, that if thou confess with thy mouth the Lord Jesus and shalt believe in thine heart that God raised Him from the dead thou shalt be saved.'

Three times in these passages he calls Jesus Lord telling us how to be saved. He says that faith in the Lord Jesus plus confession of that faith to the world brings salvation to us. God desires that we be honest with Him above everything else. Search the scriptures, read the New Testament, and if you see that I have given a germ of truth, then I urge you to do something about it. If you have been led to believe imperfectly in a divided Savior, be glad that there is still time for you to do something about it.[35]

G. Campbell Morgan

Matthew 4:17—'From that time began Jesus to preach, and to say, Repent ye, for the kingdom of heaven is at hand.'

That is the way in which Jesus always begins. His first message to men is always, Repent! He does not end there. He had much more to say to men than this ... But there is nothing Jesus can ever say until this first thing is said, and until this first thing is done.

But Jesus in this great word did not merely say, Repent...He indicated a direction. 'Repent...the kingdom of heaven is at hand.'...Jesus did not come to men and say: You are wrong, get a new idea of life. Said He: 'Repent, for the kingdom of heaven is at hand.' Herein is direction. Herein is the indication of what the change is to be.

There occur in the scriptures certain terms...the Kingdom of God, the Kingdom of Heaven, the Kingdom, the Church...What is the common principle in all these? The rule of God, the authority of the Most High over the affairs of men. The permanent principle in all these phrases is the direct right of God to govern individual life in its entirety, social life in all its relationships and national life in its purposes and its policies. **The permanent principle, that for which Jesus came, and for which He stood, is that of the**

absolute right of God to govern every man's life in every part and detail of it. This is the Kingdom of Heaven. The absolute right of God to govern social life in all its interrelationships, husband and wife, father and children, master and servant, capital and labor.

Now Jesus did not merely say, change your mind, but change your mind toward *that,* and in the phrase that indicates the direction, there flashes the light that reveals the failure. We can put the whole call into very simple phrases and words. **Change your mind about God and change your mind toward God. God is exiled, enthrone Him! That is all and that is everything**. It is a call from godlessness to Godliness...'Repent ye for the Kingdom of Heaven is at hand.'

We have lived under other lords. We have obeyed the impulses of sin, of self, of passion, of pride; we are wrong. We have wakened in the morning and we have said: What will please us today? We are wrong. Change your mind, learn to understand that you never can live, till with the break of day we say: 'Teach me to do Thy will, 0 my God.' 'Repent ye for the Kingdom of Heaven is at hand,'

It had its local application, but I take out the eternal principle; the right of God to govern human lives; to direct, immediate, positive, drastic interference with every man. This is the keynote of the preaching of Jesus.

The first thing is that we enthrone God and kiss the scepter, and bow the knee, and learn that we have no right at all except the right of being where God would have us be and doing what God would have us do.

Jesus comes to enthrone God in human life...When men repent in that direction what will happen? Their conceptions will be godly, their conduct will be godly and their character will be godly...ultimately, repentance is the turning of the back deliberately on everything that is out of harmony with the will of God. Fundamentally it is turning to God.

Repentance is turning round and facing God, recognizing the throne, submitting thereto, asking at the gates of the high place for the orders of every day and every hour. That is godly life.

Repentance is toward God, the change of the mind back toward Him, that He may be taken into account; the change of the conduct so that it may square with that master conception of life that the will of God is supreme.[36]

J.I. Packer

Evangelism means declaring a specific message...It means to present Christ Jesus Himself, the living Saviour and the reigning Lord...Evangelism means to present Jesus as Christ, God's annointed Servant, fulfilling the tasks of His appointed office as Priest and King...Evangelizing means declaring this specific message with a specific application..Evangelism means exhorting sinners to accept Christ Jesus as their Saviour, recognizing that in the most final and far reaching sense they are lost without Him. Nor is this all. Evangelism also means summoning men to receive Christ Jesus as all that He is, Lord as well as Saviour, and therefore to serve Him as their King in the fellowship of His church.

Evangelism is the issuing of a call to turn, as well as to trust; it is the delivering, not merely of a divine invitation to receive a Savior but of a divine command to repent of sin. And there is no evangelism where this specific application is not made.

Jesus has been raised and enthroned and made King and lives to save to the uttermost all who acknowledge His Lordship.

The gospel is a summons to faith and repentance. All who hear the gospel are summoned by God to repent and believe (Acts 17:30, John 6:29).

It needs to be said that faith is not a mere optimistic

feeling, any more than repentance is a mere regretful or remorseful feeling. Faith and repentance are both acts, and acts of the whole man. Faith is more than just credence; faith is essentially the casting and resting of oneself and one's confidence on the promises of mercy which Christ has given to sinners and on the Christ who gave those promises.

Equally, repentance is more than just sorrow for the past; **repentance is a change of mind and heart, a new life of denying self and serving the Saviour as King in self's place.**

More than once, Christ deliberately called attention to the radical break with the past that repentance involves. Luke 9:23,24—'If any man will come after Me, let him deny himself and take up his cross daily and follow Me...whosoever will lose his life for My sake, the same (but only he) shall save it.' Luke 14:26,33—'If any man come to Me, and hate not his father and mother and wife and children and brethren and sisters yea, and his own life also (i.e., put them all decisively second in his esteem) he cannot be my disciple...whosoever he be of you that forsaketh not all that he hath, he cannot be My disciple.'

The repentance that Christ requires of His people consists in a settled refusal to set any limit to the claims which He may make on their lives. In our own presentation of Christ's gospel therefore, we need to lay a similar stress on the cost of following Christ and make sinners face it soberly before we urge them to respond to the message of free forgiveness. In common honesty, we must not conceal the fact that free forgiveness in one sense will cost everything or else our evangelism becomes a sort of confidence trick. And where there is no clear knowledge, and hence no realistic recognition of the real claims that Christ makes, there can be no repentance, and therefore no salvation.

In the last analysis there is only one method of evangelism, namely the faithful explanation and application of the gospel message...We have to ask: is the way we present the gospel calculated to convey to people the application of the gospel and not just part of it, but the whole of it—the summons to see and know oneself as God sees and knows one, that is as a sinful creature and to face the breadth and depth of the need into which a wrong relationship with God has brought one, and to face too the cost and consequences of turning to receive Christ as Saviour and Lord. Or is it likely to be deficient here and to gloss over some of this, and to give an inadequate distorted impression of what the gospel requires...Will it leave people supposing that all they have to do is to trust Christ as a sin–bearer not realizing that they must also deny themselves and enthrone Him as their Lord (the error which we might call 'only believism')?[37]

That man should not separate what God has joined is a truth about more than marriage. God has joined the three offices of prophet (teacher), priest, and king in the mediatorial role of Jesus Christ, and directs us in the Bible to relate positively to them all. God has joined faith and repentance as two facets of response to the Savior and made it clear that turning from sin means letting ungodliness go. Biblical teaching on faith joins credence, commitment, and communion; it exhibits Christian believing as not only knowing facts about Christ, but also coming to Him in personal trust to worship, love and serve him. If we fail to keep together what God has joined together, our Christianity will be distorted.

'Lordship salvation' is a name for the view that upholds these unities. The name sounds esoteric and slightly uncouth, and its novelty would naturally suggest that the view labeled by it is a novel product, manufactured only recently. But in fact it is no more, just as it is no less, than the mainstream Protestant consensus on the nature of justifying faith, and the real novelty is the position of those who coined this name for the view they reject and who break these unities in their own teaching. That teaching reinvents the maimed account of faith given by Scottish Sandemanianism two centuries ago...Like Sandemanians, those who reject 'lordship salvation' choose to keep works out of justification. To this end, like Sandemanians again, they represent faith as simple assent to the truth about Jesus' saving role, and thus their teaching becomes vulnerable to the criticism that it exalts faith in a way that destroys faith. Simple assent to the gospel, divorced from a transforming commitment to the living Christ, is by biblical standards less than faith, and less than saving, and to elicit only assent of this kind would be to secure only false conversions. So the gospel really is at stake in this discussion, though not in the way that the opponents of 'lordship salvation' think. What is in question is the nature of faith.[38]

John Stott

What must I do to be saved? Clearly we must do something. Christianity is no mere passive acquiescence to a series of propositions, however true. We may believe in the deity and the salvation of Christ, and acknowledge ourselves to be sinners in need of His salvation; but this does not make us Christians. **We have to make a personal response to Jesus Christ, committing ourselves unreservedly to Him as our Saviour and Lord.**

Jesus never concealed the fact that His religion included a demand as well as an offer. Indeed the demand was as total as the offer was free. If He offered men His salvation, He also demanded their submission. He gave no encouragement whatever to thoughtless applicants for discipleship...He asked His first disciples and He has asked every disciple since, to give Him their thoughtful and total commitment. Nothing less than this will do.

'If any man would come after Me let him deny himself and

take up his cross and follow Me. For whoever would save his life will lose it, and whoever loses his life for My sake and the gospels will save it. For what does it profit a man to gain the whole world and forfeit his life? For what can a man give in return for his life . . .' (Mark 8:34-37).

At its simplest Christ's call was 'follow Me.' He asked men and women for their personal allegiance. He invited them to learn from Him, to obey His words and to identify themselves with His cause. Now there can be no following without a previous forsaking. To follow Christ is to renounce all lesser loyalties ....

Today, in principle, the call of the Lord Jesus has not changed. He still says, 'Follow Me,' and adds, 'whoever of you does not renounce all that he has cannot be My disciple.' In practice however, this does not mean for the majority of Christians a physical departure from their home or job. It implies rather an inner surrender of both and a refusal to allow either family or ambition to occupy the first place in our lives.

Let me be more explicit about the forsaking which cannot be separated from following Jesus Christ. First, there must be a renunciation of sin. This, in a word, is repentance. It is the first part of Christian conversion. It can in no circumstances be bypassed. Repentance and faith belong together. We cannot follow Christ without forsaking sin. Repentance is a definite turn from every thought, word, deed and habit which is known to be wrong. It is not sufficient to feel pangs of remorse or to make some kind of apology to God. Fundamentally, repentance is a matter neither of emotion nor of speech. It is an inward change of mind and attitude towards sin which leads to a change of behavior.

Second, there must be a renunciation of self. In order to follow Christ we must not only forsake isolated sins, but renounce the very principle of self–will which lies at the root of every act of sin. To follow Christ is to surrender to

78

Him the rights over our own lives. It is to abdicate the throne of our heart and do homage to Him as our King. This renunciation of self is vividly described by Jesus, in three phases:

a. It is to deny ourselves: 'if any man would come after Me let him deny himself.'...We are to disown ourselves as completely as Peter disowned Christ when he said, 'I do not know the man.' Self denial is not just giving up sweets and cigarettes, either for good, or for a period of voluntary abstinence. For it is not to deny things to myself but to deny myself to myself. It is to say no to self and yes to Christ; to repudiate self and acknowledge Christ.

b. The next phrase Jesus used is to take up the cross: 'If any man would come after Me let him deny himself and take up his cross and follow Me.'...To take up the cross is to put oneself into the position of a condemned man on his way to execution. In other words, the attitude to self which we are to adopt is that of crucifixion. Paul uses the same metaphor when he declares that those who belong to Christ Jesus have crucified the flesh (i.e. their fallen human nature) with its passions and desires. In Luke's version of this saying of Christ the adverb 'daily' is used. Every day the Christian is to die. Every day he renounces the sovereignty of his own will. Every day he renews his unconditional surrender to Jesus Christ.

c. The third expression which Jesus used to describe the renunciation of self is to lose our life: 'Whoever loses his life for My sake and the gospel's will save it.' The word for 'life' here denotes neither our physical existence nor our soul but our self. The psyche is the ego, the human personality which thinks, feels, plans, and chooses...Jesus simply used the reflexive pronoun and talked about a man forfeiting 'himself.' The man who commits himself to Christ, loses himself. This does not mean that he loses his individuality, however. His will is indeed submitted to Christ's will, but his personality is not absorbed into Christ's personality. On the contrary, when the Christian loses himself, he finds himself, he discovers his true identity.

So in order to follow Christ we have to deny ourselves, to crucify ourselves, to lose ourselves. The full inexorable demand of Jesus Christ is now laid bare. He does not call us to a sloppy halfheartedness, but to vigorous absolute commitment. He calls us to make Him our Lord. The astonishing idea is current in some circles today that we can enjoy the benefits of Christ's salvation without accepting the challenge of His sovereign Lordship. Such an unbalanced notion is not to be found in the New Testament.

To make Christ Lord is to bring every department of our public and private lives under His control. No Christian can live for himself any longer.[39]

D. Martyn Lloyd-Jones

What is the kingdom (of God)? It means in its essence, Christ's rule or the sphere and realm in which He is reigning...Wherever the reign of Christ is being manifested the kingdom of God is there...the kingdom of God is present at this moment in all who are true believers.

The kingdom of God is only present in the Church in the hearts of true believers, in the hearts of those who have submitted to Christ and in whom and among whom He reigns.

We who recognize Christ as our Lord, and in whose lives **He is reigning and ruling at this moment are in the kingdom of heaven** and the kingdom of heaven is in us. Do we belong to this kingdom? Are we ruled by Christ? Is He our King and Lord?...The kingdom of God means 'the reign of God,' 'the reign of Christ,' and **Christ is reigning today in every true Christian...Whenever Christ** is enthroned as King, the kingdom of God is come, so that while we cannot say that He is ruling over all in the world at the present time, He is certainly ruling in that way in the hearts and lives of all His people.

Matthew 7:13,14 - Strait Gate and Narrow Way

The first thing we notice is that the Christian life is narrow or strait at the very beginning. Immediately it is narrow. It is not a life which at first is fairly broad...the gate itself, the very way of entering into this life, is a narrow one.

We are told at the very outset of this way of life, before we start on it that if we would walk along it there are certain things which must be left outside, behind us. There is no room for them because we have to start by passing through a strait and narrow gate.

The first thing we leave behind us is what is called worldliness. We leave behind the crowd and the way of the world...Our Lord is warning us against the danger of an easy salvation, against the tendency to say, Just come to Christ as you are and all is going to be well. No, the gospel tells us at the outset that it is going to be difficult. It means a radical break with the world.

Yes, but still narrower and still straiter, if we really want to come into this way of life, we have to leave our 'self' outside. And it is there of course that we come to the greatest stumbling–block of all. It is one thing to leave the world, and the way of the world, but the most important thing in a sense is to leave our self outside. Have no illusion about this...for he who would enter by this gate must say goodbye to self. It is a life of self abasement, self humiliation. 'If any man will come after Me'—what happens? 'Let him deny himself (the first thing always), and take up his cross and follow Me.'

But self denial, denial of self, does not mean refraining from various pleasures and things that we may like. It means to deny our very right to ourself. We leave our self outside and go in through the gate saying, 'Yet not I but

Christ liveth in me.'

Repentance

In the same way it (the false prophet's teaching), does not emphasize repentance in any real sense. It has a very wide gate leading to salvation and a very broad way leading to heaven. You need not feel much of your own sinfulness; you need not be aware of the blackness of your own heart. You just decide for Christ and you rush in with the crowd and your name is put down and is one of the large number of decisions reported by the press.

Repentance means that you realize that you are a guilty vile sinner in the presence of God; that you deserve the wrath and punishment of God, that you are hell-bound. It means that you begin to realize that this thing called sin is in you; that you long to get rid of it, and that you turn your back on it in every shape and form. You renounce the world whatever the cost, the world in its mind and outlook as well as its practice, and you deny yourself, and take up the cross and go after Christ. Your nearest and dearest and the whole world may call you a fool, or say you have religious mania. You may have to suffer financially, but it makes no difference. That is repentance.

The false prophet does not put it like that. He heals 'the hurt of the daughter of My people slightly,' simply saying that it is all right and that you have but to come to Christ, 'follow Jesus,' or 'become a Christian.'[40]

Charles Spurgeon

Matthew 4:17—'From that time Jesus began to preach and to say Repent, for the kingdom of heaven is at hand.'

Luke 24:47—'And that repentance and remission of sins should be preached in His name among all nations beginning at Jerusalem.'

It seems from these two texts that repentance was the first subject upon which the Redeemer dwelt, and that it was the last, which, with His departing breath, He commended to the earnestness of His disciples.

Jesus Christ opens His commission by preaching repentance. What then? Did He not by this act teach us how important repentance was—so important that the very first time He opens His mouth He shall begin with 'Repent, for the kingdom of heaven is at hand'?

Did He not feel that repentance was necessary to be preached before He preached faith in Himself because the soul must first repent of sin before it will seek a Savior.

It seems to me that nothing could set forth Jesus Christ's idea of the high value of repentance more fully and effectually than the fact that He begins with it, and that He concludes with it – that He should say 'Repent', as the key note of His ministry.

There must be a true and actual abandonment of sin and a turning unto righteousness in real act and deed in every-day life.

Repentance to be sure must be entire. How many will say 'sir I will renounce this sin and the other; but there are certain darling lusts which I must keep and hold.' 0 sirs, in God's name let me tell you; it is not the giving up of one sin, nor fifty sins, which is true repentance, it is the solemn renunciation of every sin.

If thou dost harbour one of those accursed vipers in thy heart, and does give up every other, that one lust, like one leak in a ship, will sink thy soul. Think it not sufficient to give up thy outward vices, fancy it not enough to cut off the more corrupt sins of thy life; it is all or none which God demands.

Repent says He and when He bids you repent, He means repent of all thy sins, otherwise He can never accept thy repentance as real and genuine.

All sin must be given up or else you shall never have Christ: all transgression must be renounced, or else the gates of heaven must be barred against you. Let us remember then that for repentance to be sincere, it must be entire repentance.

True repentance is a turning of the heart as well as of the life; it is the giving up of the whole soul to God to be His forever and ever; it is the renunciation of the sins of the heart as well as the crimes of the life.[41]

It is not possible for us to accept Christ as our Saviour unless He also becomes our King, for a very large part of salvation consists in our being saved from sin's dominion over us, and the only way in which we can be delivered from the mastery of Satan is by becoming subject to the mastery of Christ.[42]

Handley Moule

Luke 9:23—'Whosoever will come after me let him deny himself, take up his cross daily and follow me.'

Let him deny himself—Always let us emphasize in thought and tone, that last word—let him deny himself. And what is self denial? The word is often and much mistaken in common use, as if it meant much the same as self control, the control of lower elements of our being by higher.

If a man postpones the present to the future, resolving on present loss for the sake of future gain, this is often called self denial. If a man for some high object of his own, abjures inferior pleasures, scorns delights and lives laborious days, this is often called self denial. If in the highest sphere, for the sake of rest hereafter, he inflicts on himself great unrest now, this too is often called self denial. Now the doing of such things may be wrong or may be right in itself; but it is not self denial, as the phrase is used here assuredly by our Lord. Take the New Testament and try the case by the words 'deny' and 'denial' in successive passages. I think it will be seen that self denial is not self control. In all cases at all in point, 'to deny' much more resembles in idea 'to ignore' than to control. It means to turn the back upon, to shut the eyes to, to treat as nonexistent. Let him deny himself (Luke 9:23) – let him ignore self; let him say to self – I know thee not, thou are nothing to me.

In effect may we not say the Lord's precept comes to this: the real displacement of self from the throne of life in its purposes and hopes, and the real enthronement of Another. It comes to unqualified self surrender.

We all practically understand what we mean when we speak about self and its surrender and the enthronement of Jesus Christ. We mean that whereas yesterday our aims, many of them, some of them, one of them, terminated in ourself – today, so far as we know, they all terminate in our Lord. Yesterday perhaps, in some highly refined mode, perhaps in some mode not refined, we lived at least part of our life to self, today, in full purpose, we live the whole of it to Him who died for us and rose again. Yesterday, it was very pleasant as a good thing in itself, if some action, some influence going out from us, brought back praise, spoken or unspoken, to ourselves; today, such a feeling is recognized as sin, if the pleasure terminates short of a distinct and honest reference to our Lord in us. Yesterday we were easy in the consciousness of purely personal gratification, when some intellectual success, let us say, or physical, brought credit to ourselves and stimulated self esteem. Oh how much inner force we spent in one phase or another of self esteem. But today our deliberate choice is in the other direction. We prefer with unaffected preference, that all our earnings should go straight to Another, to our Lord.

In true purpose and choice He is now the center of our whole life – not parts but the whole. We wish not to spend ten minutes irrespective of His interests, His claims, His will. This is self denial of the saints. True self denial has lodged the personality of the person as to its whole purpose working upon another center, even Jesus Christ the Lord.[43]

Charles Hodge

Romans 10:9—'That if thou shalt confess with thy mouth the Lord Jesus, and shalt believe in thine heart that God hath raised him from the dead, thou shalt be saved.'

The two requisites for salvation mentioned in this verse are confession and faith...The thing to be confessed is that Jesus Christ is Lord. That is we must openly recognize His authority to the full extent in which He is Lord; acknowledge that He is exalted above all principality and powers, that angels are made subject to Him, and of course that He is our Lord. This confession therefore, includes in it an acknowledgment of Christ's universal sovereignty and a sincere recognition of His authority over us.[44]

Kingly Office of Christ

God, as the creator and preserver of the universe, and as infinite in His being and perfections, is, in virtue of His nature, the absolute sovereign of all his creatures. This sovereignty He exercises over the material world by His wisdom and power, and over rational beings as moral ruler. From this rightful authority of God, our race revolted, and thereby became a part of the kingdom of darkness of which Satan is the head. To this kingdom the mass of mankind has ever since belonged. But God, in His grace and mercy, determined to deliver men from the consequences of their apostasy. He not only announced the coming of a Redeemer Who should destroy the power of Satan, but He at once inaugurated an antagonistic kingdom, consisting of men chosen out of the world, and through the renewing of the Holy Ghost restored in their allegiance.

The kingdom of God, therefore, as consisting of those who acknowledge, worship, love and obey Jehovah as the only living and true God, has existed in our world ever since the fall of Adam...To gather His people into this kingdom, and to carry it on to its consummation, is the end of all God's dispensations, and the purpose for which His eternal Son assumed our nature. He was born to be a king. To this end He lived and died and rose again, that He might be Lord of all those given to Him by the Father...The Scriptures constantly speak of the Messiah as a king who was to set up a kingdom into which in the end all other kingdoms were to be merged. The most familiar designation applied to Him in the Scriptures is Lord. But Lord means proprietor and ruler; and when used of God and Christ, it means absolute proprietor and sovereign ruler...Nothing, therefore, is more certain, according to the Scriptures, than that Christ is a king; and consequently, if we would retain the truth concerning Him and His work, He must be so regarded in our theology and religion.

He is the king of every believing soul. He translates it from the kingdom of darkness. He brings it into subjection to Himself. He rules in and reigns over it. Every believer recognizes Christ as His absolute Sovereign; Lord of his inward, as well as of his outward life. He yields to Him the entire subjection of the reason, of the conscience, and of the heart. He makes Him the object of reverence, love and obedience...To acquit himself as a good soldier of Jesus Christ, to spend and be spent in His service and in the promotion of His kingdom, becomes the governing purpose of his life.

The laws of this kingdom require first and above all, faith in Jesus Christ, the sincere belief that He is the Son of God and the Saviour of the world, and cordial submission to Him and to trust in Him as our prophet, priest and king. With this faith is united supreme love. 'He that loveth father or mother more than me, is not worthy of me: and he that loveth son or daughter more than me is not worthy of me...He that findeth his life, shall lose it; and he that loseth his life for my sake shall find it' (Matt. 10:37,39). 'If any man come to me, and hate not his father, and mother, and wife, and children, and brethren, and sisters, yea, and his own life also, he cannot be my disciples' (Luke 14:26). 'If any man love not the Lord Jesus Christ, let him be anathema maranatha' (1 Cor. 16:22). With this supreme love are to be connected all the other religious affections. Christians are the worshippers of Christ.

But if we are to recognize Christ as Thomas did (John 20:28), as our Lord and our God, then of course we are bound not only to worship, but to obey him. We stand to Him in the same relation that a slave does to his master, except that our subjection to Him is voluntary and joyful. We belong to Him, not only as the Creator, being His creatures, but also as the Theanthropos, being purchased by His blood (I Cor. 6:19-20). His will, and not our own, must govern our conduct, and determine the use we make of our powers. All we gain, whether of knowledge, wealth, or influence, is His. He, and not we ourselves, is the object or end of our living. It is Christ for believers to live. His glory and the advancement of His kingdom, are the only legitimate objects to which they can devote their powers or resources; the only ends consistent with their relation to Christ, and the full enjoyment of the blessedness which membership in His kingdom secures.

The kingdom of Christ is not a democracy, nor an aristocracy, but truly a kingdom of which Christ is absolute sovereign.[45]

Faith and repentance are graces not only alike indispensable, but they cannot exist separately. Repentance is a turning from sin unto God, through Jesus Christ, and faith is the acceptance of Christ in order to our return to

God...In the ordinary religious sense of the term, it (repentance) is a turning from sin unto God...That repentance, therefore, which is unto life, is a turning; not a being driven away from sin by fear and stress of conscience, but a forsaking it as evil and hateful, with sincere sorrow, humility, and confession; and a returning unto God, because he is good and willing to forgive, with a determination to live in obedience to his commandments...Our repentance needs to be repented of, unless it leads us to confession and restitution in cases of private injury; unless it causes us to forsake not merely outward sins, which attract the notice of others, but those which lie concealed in the heart; unless it makes us choose the service of God, as that which is right and congenial, and causes us to live not for ourselves, but for Him who loved us and gave Himself for us...The salvation offered in the gospel, though it be a salvation of sinners, is also a salvation from sin...**No man, therefore, can be saved who does not, by repentance, forsake his sins. This is itself a great part of salvation. The inward change of heart from the love and service of sin to the love and service of God, is the great end of the death of Christ...A salvation for sinners, therefore, without repentance, is a contradiction.**

Hence it is that repentance is the burden of evangelical preaching. Our Saviour himself, when he began to preach, said, 'Repent: for the kingdom of heaven is at hand.' And when he came into Galilee preaching the gospel, he said, 'The time is fulfilled, and the kingdom of God is at hand: repent ye, and believe the gospel.' The commission which he gave his apostles was, 'That repentance and remission of sins should be preached in his name among all nations.' In the execution of this commission his disciples went forth and preached, 'Repent ye, and be converted, that your sins May be blotted out, when the times of refreshing shall come from the presence of the Lord. Paul, in the account which he gave Agrippa of his preaching, said that he showed first unto them of Damascus, and at Jerusalem, and throughout all the coasts of Judea, and then to the Gentiles, that they should repent and turn to God, and do works meet for repentance. And he called upon the elders at Ephesus to bear witness that he had taught 'publically, and from house to house, testifying both to the Jews, and also to the Greeks, repentance toward God, and faith toward our Lord Jesus Christ.'

Repentance, then, is the great, immediate, and pressing duty of all who hear the gospel. They are called upon to forsake their sins, and return unto God through Jesus Christ. The neglect of this duty is the rejection of salvation. For, as we have seen, unless we repent we must perish...Though repentance is a duty, it is no less the gift of God.[46]

Griffith Thomas

Romans 14:9—'For this purpose Christ died and rose again that He might be Lord both of the living and the dead.'

Our relation to Christ is based on His death and resurrection and this means His Lordship. Indeed the Lordship of Christ over the lives of His people was the very purpose for which He died and rose again. We have to acknowledge Christ as our Lord. **Sin is rebellion, and it is only as we surrender to Him as our Lord** that **we receive pardon from Him as our Savior.** We have to admit Him to reign on the throne of the heart, and it is only when He is glorified in our hearts as King that the Holy Spirit enters and abides.[47]

A.A. Hodge

The Scriptures make it plain that the condition of its effectual application (redemption) is an act of faith, involving real spiritual repentance and the turning from sin and the acceptance and self–appropriation of Christ and of His redemption as the only remedy...From within, the God–man reigns supreme in every Christian heart. **It is impossible to accept Christ as our Sacrifice and Priest without at the same time cordially accepting Him** as our Prophet, absolutely submitting our understanding to His teaching and accepting Him **as our King, submitting implicitly our hearts and wills and lives to His sovereign control.** Paul delights to call himself the doulos–purchased servant of Jesus Christ. Every Christian spontaneously calls Him our LORD Jesus. His will is our law, His love our motive, His glory our end. To obey His will, to work in His service, to fight His battles, to triumph in His victories, is our whole life and joy. [48]

Now, every Christian who really has experienced the grace of Christ must, unless very greatly prejudiced, recognize the fact that this work of sanctification is the *end* and the *crown* of the whole process of salvation. We insist upon and put forward distinctly the great doctrine of justification as a means to an end. It is absolutely necessary as the condition of that faith which is the necessary source of regeneration and sanctification; and every person who is a Christian must recognize the fact that not only will it issue in sanctification, but it must begin in sanctification. This element must be recognized as characteristic of the Christian experience from the first to the last. And any man who thinks that he is a Christian, and that he has accepted Christ for justification when he did not at the same time accept Christ for sanctification, is miserably deluded in that very experience. He is in danger of falling under the judgment of which Paul admonishes when he speaks of the wrath of God coming down from heaven upon all ungodliness and unrighteousness of men, and with special reference to those who 'hold the truth in unrighteousness.'[49]

A.W. Pink

The word of God teaches plainly that in this dispensation, equally with preceding ones, **God requires a sincere and deep repentance before He pardons any sinner.**

Repentance is absolutely necessary for salvation, just as necessary as is faith in the Lord Jesus Christ. 'Except ye repent, ye shall all likewise perish' (Luke 13:3). 'Then hath God also to the Gentiles granted repentance unto life' (Acts 11: 18). 'For godly sorrow worketh repentance to salvation not to be repented of' (2 Car. 7: 10). It is impossible to frame language more explicit than that. Therefore in view of these verses and others, we cannot but sorrowfully regard those who are now affirming that repentance is not in this dispensation, essential unto salvation, as being deceivers of souls, blind leaders of the blind.

In repentance sin is the thing to be repented of and sin is a transgression of the law (I John 3:4). And the first and chief thing required by the law is supreme love to God. Therefore, the lack of supreme love to God, the heart's disaffection for His character and rebellion against Him (Rom. 8:7) is our great wickedness, of which we have to repent.

What is sin? Sin is saying...I disallow His (God's) right to govern me. I am going to be lord of myself. Sin is rebellion against the Majesty of heaven...The language of every sinner's heart is, I care not what God requires, I am going to have my own way. I care not what be God's claims upon me, I refuse to submit to His authority.

The Lord Jesus taught and constantly pressed the same truth. His call was 'Repent ye and believe the gospel' (Mark 1:15). **The gospel cannot be savingly believed until there is genuine repentance**.

When the gospel first comes to the sinner it finds him in a state of apostasy from God, both as sovereign Ruler and as our supreme good, neither obeying and glorifying Him, nor enjoying and finding satisfaction in Him. Hence the demand for 'repentance toward God' before 'faith toward our Lord Jesus Christ' (Acts 20:21). True repentance toward God removes this dissatisfaction of our minds and hearts toward Him, under both these characters. In saving repentance the whole soul turns to Him and says: I have been a disloyal and rebellious creature. I have scorned Thy high authority and most rightful law. I will live no longer thus. I desire and determine with all my might to serve and obey Thee as my only Lord. I subject myself unto Thee, to submit to Thy will...Repentance...is the perception that God has the right to rule and govern me, and of my refusal to submit unto Him...As the Holy Spirit sets before me the loveliness of the divine character, as I am enabled to discern the exalted excellency of God, then I begin to perceive that to which He is justly entitled, namely, the homage of my heart, the unrestricted love of my soul, the complete surrender of my whole being to Him.

Many are the scriptures which set forth this truth, that there must be a forsaking of sin before God will pardon offenders.

He must be crowned Lord of all or He will not be Lord at all. There must be the complete heart–renunciation of all that stands in competition with Him. He will brook no rival.

Thus repentance is the negative side of conversion. Conversion is a whole–hearted turning unto God, but there cannot be a turning unto, without a turning from. Sin must be forsaken ere we can draw nigh unto the Holy One. As it is written, 'Ye turned to God from idols to serve (live for) the living and true God' (I Thess. 1:9).

Make no mistake upon the point...it is turn or burn; turn from your course of self will and self pleasing, turn in brokenheartedness to God, seeking His mercy in Christ, turn with full purpose to please and serve Him, or be tormented day and night forever and ever in the lake of fire.[50]

James Montgomery Boice

There is a fatal defect in the life of Christ's church in the twentieth century: a lack of true discipleship. Discipleship means forsaking everything to follow Christ. But for many of today's supposed Christians—perhaps the majority—it is the case that while there is much talk about Christ and even much furious activity, there is actually very little following of Christ Himself. And that means in some circles there is very little genuine Christianity. Many who fervently call Him 'Lord, Lord' are not Christians (Matthew 7:21)...There are several reasons that the situation I have described is common in today's church. The first is a defective theology that has crept over us like a deadening fog. This theology separates faith from discipleship and grace from obedience. It teaches that Jesus can be received as one's Savior without being received as one's Lord...Discipleship in not a supposed second step in Christianity, as if one first became a believer in Jesus and then, if he chooses, a disciple. From the beginning, discipleship is involved in what it means to be a Christian....Is 'faith' minus commitment a true biblical faith?...If faith without works is dead—how much truer is it that faith without commitment is dead...True faith involves these elements: knowledge...heart response...and commitment, without which 'faith' is no different from the assent of the demons who 'believe...and shudder' (James 2:19). [51]

William Hendriksen

Mark 8:34—'Whosoever will come after me, let him deny himself, and take up his cross, and follow me.'

To come after Jesus means to attach oneself to Him as His disciple. What then must a person do in order to be considered a true disciple? Well, if he wishes to come after Me, says Jesus, then first, he must deny himself; that is, he must once for all say farewell to the old self, the self as it is apart from regenerating grace.

Secondly, he must take up his cross. The underlying figure is that of a condemned man who is forced to take up and carry his own cross to the place of execution.

Finally, he must follow and keep on following Jesus. Here, following the Master means trusting Him (John 3:16), walking in His footsteps (I Peter 2:21), and obeying His commands (John 15:14) out of gratitude for salvation in Him (Eph. 4:32-5:2).

Together the three indicate true conversion, followed by life-long sanctification.[52]

In the next three verses...the obligation to be converted, etc., and the reward that results are brought into sharp contrast with the loss experienced by those who refuse to deny themselves, to take up their cross, and to follow Jesus...Accordingly, with an implied 'Let him not refuse,' there follows...For whoever would save his life shall lose it, but whoever loses his life for may sake, he shall save it. Meaning: the individual who would—or 'should wish to'— save his life shall lose it. Exactly what is it that he wishes to save? Answer: his life, that is, himself...This man clings to that sinful life of his, holding on to it tenaciously...On the other hand, whoever loses his life 'for my sake,' he shall save it. One loses his life in the present sense by devoting oneself completely to Christ, to the service of those in need, to the gospel (Cf. Mark 8:35). **Note that Christ lays claim to absolute devotion. This proves that he regards himself as Lord of all,** and that the evangelist was fully aware of this! The person who offers this devotion saves his life, that is, his soul, or as we can also say, *himself*...**It is only by losing** oneself—looking away from self in order to serve the Master and his 'little ones' (Cf. Matt. 25:40)—that one can ever be saved...For the sinner salvation is impossible apart from obedience to this rule.[53]

R.C.H. Lenski

Mark 8:34—'Whosoever will come after me, let him deny himself, and take up his cross, and follow me.'

To deny means to refuse association and companionship with, to disown. And the one to be disowned and denied is...self—and that means self altogether, not merely some portion, some special habit or desire, some outward practice.

As Peter afterwards denied Jesus by saying, 'I know not the man,' so must you say this to your self: 'I disown you completely.'

This is not self denial in the current sense of the word but true conversion, the very first essential of the Christian life. The heart sees all the sin of self and the damnation and death bound up in this sin and turns away from it in utter dismay and seeks refuge in Christ alone. Self is thus cast out and Christ enters in; henceforth you live, not unto yourself, but unto Christ who died for you.

So you are to deny your very own self, and enter the new relation with Christ.[54]

John Calvin

The Hebrew word for repentance is derived from conversion or return; the Greek word from change of mind or of intention. And the thing itself corresponds closely to the etymology of both words.

The meaning is that, departing from ourselves we are to turn to God, and having taken off our former mind, we put on a new. On this account, in my judgment, repentance can thus be well defined: it is the true turning of our life to God, a turning that arises from a pure and earnest fear of Him, and it consists in the mortification of our flesh and of the old man, and in the vivification of the spirit.

When we call repentance a turning of the life to God we require a transformation, not only in outward works, but in the soul itself. Only when it puts off its old nature does it bring forth the fruits of works in harmony with its renewal.

Repentance consists of two parts: namely, mortification of the flesh and vivification of the spirit.

The prophets express it clearly although simply and rudely in accordance with the capacity of the carnal folk when they say 'Cease to do evil and do good' (Ps. 36:8,3,27).

For when they call men from evil they demand the destruction of the whole flesh which is full of evil and perversity. It is a very hard and difficult thing to put off ourselves and to depart from our inborn disposition. Nor can we think of the flesh as completely destroyed unless we have wiped out whatever we have from ourselves. But since all emotions of the flesh are hostility against God (Rom. 8:7), the first step toward obeying His law is to deny ourselves our own nature. Surely, as we are naturally turned away from God, unless self denial precedes, we shall never approach that which is right. Therefore, we are very often enjoined to put off the old man, to denounce the world and the flesh, to bid our evil desires farewell, to be renewed in the spirit of our mind. (Eph. 4:22,23)

From mortification we infer that we are not conformed to the fear of God and do not learn the rudiments of piety, unless we are violently slain by the sword of the Spirit and brought to nought. **As if God had declared that for us to be reckoned among His children our common nature must die.**[55]

D. James Kennedy

'I tell you, Nay: but, except ye repent, ye shall all likewise perish.' These are the words of Jesus Christ concerning repentance. In a way, it's a strange doctrine because repentance itself will not save you. Yet you cannot be saved without it ...

While many churches ignore this doctrine, the Bible gives it considerable emphasis. Both Old and New Testaments call upon men to repent. Noah was a preacher of righteousness, calling men to leave their wicked ways and turn unto God. All the prophets were preachers of repentance. In fact, Nahum's name comes from a root meaning repentance. Both the major and minor prophets called people to repent. John the Baptist said: 'Repent... who hath warned you to flee from the wrath to come? Bring forth therefore fruits meet for repentance.'

When Christ reached His thirtieth year (the time for the priest to begin his priestly function), our Great High Priest was baptized and began His work as prophet and priest. How did Jesus begin His ministry? Matthew says: 'From that time Jesus began to preach, and to say, Repent...' The burden of His heart and ministry for this world of sinners was: Repent! 'Except ye repent, ye shall all likewise perish.' Many of His parables, such as the prodigal son, dealt with the subject of repentance. After Jesus' resurrection, on the road to Emmaus, He said to the two: 'Thus it is written, and thus it behoved Christ to suffer, and to rise from the dead the third day: And that repentance and remission of sins should be preached in his name among all nations, beginning at Jerusalem.' Christ began, continued, and ended His ministry with the same word—repent!

At Pentecost, when the Spirit of God was poured out and the church began its distinctively Christian ministry, Peter preached the first sermon. After the people were reminded what God had done, they said: 'What must we do?' And

Peter said: 'Repent.'

Paul said he was called by God to preach that men should exercise repentance toward God and faith in the Lord Jesus Christ. 'And the times of this ignorance God winked at; but now commandeth all men every where to repent.' The letters to the churches in the Book of Revelation abound in commands to repent. Eight times in these letters Jesus walks among his churches, symbolic of the churches of all times, and says: 'Repent...or else I will come unto thee quickly, and will remove thy candlestick out of his place.' Fifty–three times in the New Testament men are called to repent or told they must have repentance.

Repentance and faith are inseparable in Scripture. There can be no genuine repentance without faith. And there is no genuine faith without repentance. The two go together as heads and tails on one coin.

Because the human soul is made up of mind, heart, and will, all three must become involved in true faith and repentance. We must intellectually grasp that sin, because of its heinousness, will inevitably be punished by God. We must also intellectually grasp and understand the divine remedy for sin. We must come to know the way of salvation as it has been divinely appointed by God and must not be deluded by some false plan of salvation of our own making. We must understand it is only through Christ, His grace, and death on the cross that we have eternal hope. But even understanding will not be sufficient. It must go beyond the mind to the heart, to the affection. We must come to God with a contrite heart...'A broken and contrite heart, 0 God, thou wilt not despise.'

There are others who have been reared in the church and suppose themselves to be Christian but have never by any act of their will renounced their sins and turned to Jesus Christ. But nothing less will suffice for repentance! It is only as we see the awfulness of our own sin and truly desire in our hearts to turn from them and embrace the Savior, that

God accepts our repentance.

Have you repented of your sins or are you deluded into believing that you can live in sin and then in heaven? The Word of Christ to you is unmistakable....Jesus Christ says: 'Except ye repent, ye shall all likewise perish.'[56]

J.B. Lightfoot

Faith is not an intellectual assent, nor a sympathetic sentiment merely. **It is the absolute surrender of self to the will of a Being who has a right to command this surrender.** It is this which places men in personal relation to God, which (in St. Paul's language) justifies them before God. For it touches the springs of their actions; it fastens not on this or that detail of conduct, but extends throughout the whole sphere of moral activity, and thus it determines their character as responsible beings in the sight of God.[57]

Henry C. Thiessen

The Scriptures appeal to man to turn to God (Prov. 1:23; Isa. 31:6,59:20; Ezek. 14:6, 18:32, 33:9-11)...Conversion is that turning to God and it represents the human response to the call of God. It consists of two elements: repentance and faith.

Repentance

The importance of repentance is not always recognized as it should be. Some call upon the unsaved to accept Christ and to believe without ever showing the sinner that he is lost and needs a savior. But the Scriptures lay much stress on the preaching of repentance.

Repentance was the message of the Old Testament prophets (Deut. 30: 10-1 2 Kings 17:13; Jer. 8:6, Ezek. 14:6, 18:30). It was the keynote of the preaching of John the

Baptist (Matt. 3:2; Mark 11:15), of Christ (Matt. 4:17; Luke 13:3-5), of the twelve as such (Mark 6:12), and in particular of Peter on the day of Pentecost (Acts 2:38; cf. 3:19). It was also fundamental to the preaching of Paul (Acts 20:21; 26:20).

The dispensational change has not made repentance unnecessary in this age; it is definitely a command to all men (Acts 17:30). This is what Paul said at Athens, the farthest removed from a Jewish environment. Repentance is something in which all heaven is supremely interested (Luke 15:7, 10; 24:46f). **It is the fundamental of fundamentals (Matt. 21:32; Heb. 6: 1) because it is an absolute condition of salvation** (Luke 13:2-5).

Repentance is essentially a change of mind, taking the word in a broad sense. It has, however, three aspects: an intellectual, an emotional, and a volitional aspect

1) The intellectual element – This implies a change of view. It is a change of view with regard to sin, God and self.

2) The emotional element – This implies a change of feeling. Sorrow for sin and a desire for pardon are aspects of repentance.

3) The volitional element – This element implies a change of will, disposition and purpose. This is the inward turning from sin.

Repentance is not a satisfaction rendered to God, but a condition of the heart necessary before we can believe unto salvation. Furthermore true repentance never exists apart from faith.. Conversely we may say that true faith never exists without repentance. The two are inseparably bound together.

Faith

What then is faith? ... In conversion, faith is the turning of the soul to God as repentance is the turning of the soul from sin ... We may say that the scriptures represent faith as an act of the heart. It therefore involves an intellectual, an emotional and a volitional change. Men believe with the heart to be saved (Romans 10:9f). The scriptures emphasize the intellectual aspect of faith in such references as Psalm 9:10, John 2:23f and Romans 10:14. Nicodemus had faith in this sense of the term when he came to Jesus (John 3:2) and the demons we are told, believe, for they know the facts concerning God (James 2:19). It is no doubt in this sense also that Simon Magus believed (Acts 8:13) for there are no indications that he repented and appropriated Christ.

We conclude therefore that faith must be more than intellectual assent. A man is not saved unless his faith has all three of these elements in it (emotional, intellectual, volitional). The voluntary element, however, is so comprehensive that it presupposes the other two. Certainly no one can be saved who does not voluntarily appropriate Christ. **The voluntary element includes the surrender of the heart to God and the appropriation of Christ as Saviour.** The former is brought out in such scriptures as 'Give me you heart my son and let your eyes delight in my ways' (Prov. 23:26). 'Come to me all who are weary and heavy laden and I will give you rest. Take my yoke upon you and learn of me' (Matt. 11:28). 'If anyone comes to me and does not hate his own father and mother and wife and children and brothers and sister, yes, and even his own life, he cannot be my disciple' (Luke 14:26).

That the Greek term *pisteuo* (to believe or trust) is used in the sense of surrender and commitment is seen in such statements as: 'But Jesus on his part was not entrusting himself to them for he knew all men' (John 2:24). 'They were entrusted with the gospel' (Gal. 2:7).

The scriptures frequently emphasize that men should count the cost before deciding to follow Christ (Matt. 8:19–22, Luke 14:26-33).

The thought of surrender is also implied in the

exhortation to accept Jesus as Lord. The command is, 'Believe on the Lord Jesus Christ' (Acts 16:31). And we must 'confess Jesus as Lord to be saved' (Rom. 10:9) **To believe in Him as Lord is to recognize Him as Lord, and we cannot recognize Him as Lord until we ourselves abdicate.**

This note of faith is often overlooked or even referred to as a later time of consecration, but the scriptures connect it with the initial experience of salvation.[58]

Augustus H. Strong

Conversion is that voluntary change in the mind of the sinner, in which he turns, on the one hand, from sin, and on the other hand to Christ. The former or negative element in conversion, namely, the turning from sin, we denominate repentance. The latter or positive element in conversion, namely, the turning to Christ, we denominate faith.

Repentance

Repentance is that voluntary change in the mind of the sinner in which he turns from sin. Being essentially a change of mind, it involves a change of view, a change of feeling and a change of purpose. We may therefore analyze repentance into three constituents, each succeeding term of which includes and implies the one preceding:
A) An intellectual element—a change of view— recognition of sin as involving personal guilt, defilement, and helplessness.
B) An emotional element—change of feeling—sorrow for sin as committed against goodness and justice and therefore hateful to God and hateful to itself.
C) A voluntary element—a change of purpose—inward turning from sin and disposition to seek pardon and cleansing. This includes and implies the two preceding elements, and is therefore the most important aspect

of repentance. It is indicated in the Scripture term metanoia (Acts 2:38; Rom. 2:4).

The idea of metanoia is abandonment of sin rather than sorrow for sin—an act of the will rather than a state of the sensibility...It is repentance from sin, not of sin, nor for sin. In further explanation of the Scripture representations we remark:

a) That repentance, in each and all aspects, is wholly an inward act, not to be confounded with the change of life which proceeds from it.

b) That repentance is only a negative condition, and not a positive means of salvation.

c) That true repentance never exists except in conjunction with faith.

d) That, conversely, where ever there is true faith, there is true repentance also.

Since repentance and faith are but different sides or aspects of the same acts of turning, faith is as inseparable from repentance as repentance is from faith.

Faith

Faith is that voluntary change in the mind of the sinner in which he turns to Christ. Being essentially a change of mind, it involves a change of view, a change of feeling and a change of purpose.

We may therefore analyze faith also into three constituents, each succeeding term of which includes and implies the preceding (intellectual, emotional and volitional). **The voluntary element is trust in Christ as Lord and Savior**, or in other words, to distinguish its two aspects:

a. **Surrender of the soul, as guilty and defiled to Christ's governance** (Matt. 11:28,29, John 8:12, Acts 16:3 1, John 2:24, Romans 3:2, Gal. 2:7). "Pistis" equals trustful self surrender to God (Meyer). In this surrender of the soul to Christ's governance we have the guarantee that the gospel salvation is not an unmoral trust which permits continuance in sin. Aside from the fact that saving faith is only the obverse side of true repentance, **the very nature of faith as submission to Christ,** the embodied law of God and source of spiritual life, makes a life of obedience and virtue to be its natural and necessary result.

Faith is not only a declaration of dependence, it is also a vow of allegiance. The sick man's faith in his physician is shown not simply by trusting him, but by obeying him. Doing what the doctor says is the very proof of trust. Faith is self surrender to the Great Physician and a leaving of our case in His hands. But it is also the taking of His prescriptions and the active following of His directions.

Faith is not simple receptiveness. It gives itself as well as receives Christ. It is not mere passivity; it is also self committal. There are great things received in faith, but nothing is received by the man who does not first give himself to Christ. While faith is the act of the whole man, and intellect, affections and will are involved; in it, will is the all–inclusive and most important of its elements. No other exercise of will is such a revelation of our being and so decisive of our destiny.

The voluntary element of faith is illustrated in marriage. Here, one party pledges the future in permanent self surrender, commits oneself to another person in confidence that this future, with all its new revelations of character will only justify the decision made.

b. **Reception and appropriation of Christ as the source of pardon and spiritual life** (John 1: 12, 4:14, 6:53, 20:3 1, Rev. 3:20).

Faith then is a taking of Christ as both Lord and Savior and it includes both appropriation of Christ and consecration to Christ.[59]

Louis Berkhof

True saving faith is a faith that has its seat in the heart and is rooted in the regenerate life...In speaking of the different elements of faith we should not lose sight of the fact that faith is an activity of man as a whole, and not any part of man...In order to obtain a proper conception of faith, it is necessary to distinguish between the various elements which it comprises.

A) An intellectual element (notitia). There is an element of knowledge in faith...The knowledge of faith consists in a positive recognition of the truth, in which man accepts as true whatsoever God says in His word, and especially what He says respecting the deep depravity of man and the redemption which is in Christ Jesus. Over against Rome the position must be maintained that this sure knowledge belongs to the essence of faith; and in opposition to such theologians as Sandeman, Wardlaw, Alexander, Chalmers, and others, that a mere intellectual acceptance of the truth is not the whole of faith.

B) An emotional element (Assensus). When one embraces Christ by faith, he has a deep conviction of the truth and reality of the object of faith, feels that it meets an important need in his life, and is conscious of an absorbing interest in it – and this is assent.

C) A volitional element (fiducia). This is the crowning element of faith. Faith is not merely a matter of the intellect, nor of the intellect and the emotions combined; it is also a matter of the will, determining the direction of the soul, an act of the soul going out towards its object and appropriating this. Without this activity the object of faith, which the sinner recognizes as true and real and entirely applicable to his present needs, remains outside of him. And in saving faith it is a matter of life and death that the object be appropriated. This third element consists in a personal trust in Christ as Saviour and Lord, including the surrender of the soul as guilty and defiled to Christ, and a recognition and appropriation of Christ as the source of pardon and of spiritual life.[60]

The special act of faith consists in receiving Christ and resting on Him as He is presented in the gospel...Strictly speaking, it is not the act of faith as such, but rather that which is received by faith, which justifies and therefore saves the sinner.[61]

Conversion consists in repentance and faith, so that faith is really a part of conversion...Logically, repentance and the knowledge of sin precede the faith that yields to Christ in trusting love.[62]

John Murray

The Nature (of faith)—its Constituitive Elements:

A) **Notitia.** Faith respects an object and in this case Christ. But there can be no trust without knowledge of the person in whom trust is reposed. We do not trust any person unless we know something about him and, more particularly, things pertaining to that in respect of which we have confidence. So it is with Christ.

B) **Assensus.** This has two aspects: a) Intellective...The information conveyed is recognized by us to be true...b) Emotive...It is truth believed as applicable to ourselves, as supremely vital and important for us. Saving faith cannot be in exercise unless there is a recognition of correspondence between our needs and the provision of the gospel. Knowledge passes into conviction.

C) **Fiducia**. Saving faith is not simply assent to propositions of truth respecting Christ, and defining the person that he is, nor simply assent to a proposition respecting his sufficiency to meet and satisfy our deepest needs. Faith must rise to trust, and trust that consists in entrustment to him. In faith there is the engagement of person to person in the inner movement of the whole man to receive and rest upon Christ alone for salvation. It means the abandonment of confidence in our own or any human resources in a totality act of self–commitment to Christ.

This fiducial character, consisting in entrustment to Christ for salvation, serves to correct misapprehensions. Faith is not belief that we have been saved, nor belief that Christ has saved us, nor even belief that Christ died for us. It is necessary to appreciate the point of distinction. **Faith is in its essence commitment to Christ that we may be saved**. The premise of that commitment is that we are unsaved and we believe on Christ in order that we may be saved...It is to lost sinners that Christ is offered, and the demand of that overture is simply and solely that we commit ourselves to him in order that we may be saved.

Faith is a whole–souled movement of intelligent, consenting, and confiding self–commitment, and all these elements or ingredients coalesce to make faith what it is. Intellect, feeling and will converge upon Christ in those exercises which belong properly to these distinct though inseparable aspects of psychial activity.[63]

Justification is by faith and therefore can never be separated from it. **What is this faith? It is trust in Christ for salvation from sin. It is to contradict the very nature of faith to regard it as anything else than a sin–hating, sin–condemning, and sin–renouncing principle. Since faith is a whole–souled movement of trust in Christ its very spring and motive is salvation from sin**...As regeneration is the fountain of faith and faith is the logical pre-condition of justification, we can never think of justification apart from regeneration. And, again, **the faith that justifies is faith conjoined with repentance**.[64]

All along the line of obligations, overtures and priviledges of the divine call, there is an utter incongruity between the condition of the called and the calling. The response to the call is a whole–souled movement of loving subjection and trust in God. It is a totality of a man's soul...It is a turning to God with the whole heart and soul and strength and mind.[65]

According to the more classic protestant position faith is simply the instrument whereby justification is appropriated. The faith in view is not faith in justification but faith in Christ, the faith directed to him and commitment to him for salvation (cf. *Westminster Confession* XI, iv)...Faith has as its specific quality the receiving and resting of self-abandonment and totality of self-commitment.[66]

Faith is always joined with repentance, love and hope. A faith severed from these is not the faith of the contrite and therefore it is not the faith that justifies. But it is faith alone that justifies because its specific quality is to find our all in Christ and his righteousness.[67]

R.L. Dabney

Faith embraces Christ substantially in all His offices. This must be urged as of prime practical importance. Dr. Owen has in one place very incautiously said, that saving faith in its first movement embraces Christ only in His priestly, or propitiatory work. This teaching is far too common, at least by implication, in our pulpits. Its result is 'temporary' faith, which embraces Christ for impunity only, instead of deliverance from sin. Our Catechism defines faith, as embracing Christ 'as He is offered in the gospel.' Our Confession (chap. xiv.2), says: 'the principal acts of saving faith are accepting, receiving, and resting upon Christ alone for justification, sanctification and eternal life.' How Christ is offered us in the gospel, may be seen in Matt. 1:21; 1 Cor. 1:30; Eph. 5:25-27; Titus 1:14. The tendency of human selfishness is ever to degrade Christ's sacrifice into a mere expedient for bestowing impunity. The pastor can never be too explicit in teaching that this is a travesty of the gospel; and that no one rises above the faith of the stony–ground hearer, until he desires and embraces Christ as deliverer from the depravity of sin, as well as hell.

Godly sorrow for sin must be presupposed or implied in the first actings of faith, because faith embraces Christ as a Saviour from sin...Surely the Scriptures do not present Christ to our faith only, or even mainly, as a way of impunity. See Matt. i:21; Acts iii:26; Titus ii:14. As we have pointed out, the most characteristic defect of a dead faith, is, that it would quite heartily embrace Christ as God's provision for immunity from sin: but God offers Him to faith for a very different purpose, viz: for restoration to holiness, including immunity from wrath as one of the secondary consequences thereof.

The first and most urgent want of the soul, convicted of its guilt and danger, is impunity. Hence, the undue prevalence, even in preaching, of that view of Christ which holds Him up as expiation only. We have seen that even an Owen could be guilty of what I regard as the dangerous statement, that the true believer, in embracing Christ, first receives Him only in His priestly office! The faith which does no more than this, is but partial, and can bear but spurious fruits. Is not this the explanation of much of that defective and spurious religion with which the Church is cursed? The man who is savingly wrought upon by the Holy Ghost, is made to feel that his bondage under corruption is an evil as inexorable and dreadful as the penal curse of the law. He needs and desires Christ in His prophetic and kingly offices, as much as in His priestly. His faith 'receives Him as He is offered to us in the gospel'; that is, as a 'Saviour of His people from their sins.'[68]

The manner in which faith and repentance are coupled together in Scripture plainly shows that, as faith is implicitly present in repentance, so repentance is implicitly in faith...True faith is obediential: it involves the will: it has moral quality: but its receptive nature is what fits it to be the organ of our justification.[69]

Saving faith versus temporary faith: The efficient cause of saving faith is effectual calling, proceeding from God's immutable election...That of temporary faith is the common call. The subject of saving faith is a 'good heart;' a regenerate soul: that of temporary faith is a stony soul...Their objects are different: saving faith embracing Christ as He is offered in the gospel, a Saviour from sin to holiness: and temporary faith embracing only the impunity and enjoyments of the Christian.[70]

True faith is obediential: it involves the will.'[71]

Repentance

'Repentance unto life is an evangelical grace, the doctrine whereof is to be preached by every minister of the gospel, as well as that of faith in Christ' (Conf. xv,1). The brevity, and in some cases neglect, with which this prominent subject is treated by many systems, is surprising and reprehensible...Of what should man repent? The general answer, of course, must be: Of all sin...Of the corruption of nature, of the concupiscence and inordinate desire of our hearts, it is our duty to repent, to feel blameworthy for them, to sorrow for, and to strive against them, just as of actual transgression; for this not only our guilt (imputed), but our proper sin. Again, Conf., xv.5, 'Men ought not only to repent of their sinfulness, both of heart and life, as a general quality, but also of particular sins, so far as they are known, with a particular repentance.'

The relations of faith and repentance *inter se*, as to the order of production, are important to an understanding of conversion. Both these graces are the exercises of a regenerate heart alone; they presuppose the new birth. Now, Calvin, with perhaps the current of Calvinistic divines, says, that 'repentance not only immediately follows faith, but is produced by it.' Again: 'When we speak of faith as the origin of repentance, we dream not of any space of time which it employs in producing it; but we intend to signify that a man cannot truly devote himself to repentance, unless he knows himself to be of God.' And this, he adds, only becomes known by appropriating faith...Now there is a fair sense in which all this is true; and that, no doubt, the sense in which it commended itself to the minds of those great and good men. But there is also a great danger of holding it in an erroneous and mischevious sense. In what we have to say, guarding these views, let us premise that we make no priority of time in the order of repentance and faith; and no gap of duration between the birth of the one or the other. Either implies the other in that sense. Nor do we dream of the existence of such a thing as a penitent unbeliever, nor suppose that there is any other means of producing repentance than the preaching of the gospel. Repentance can exist nowhere except where God works it. In rational adults He works it only by means, and that means is the gospel revelation; none other. Nor do we retract one word of what we said as to the prime efficiency of the doctrine of the cross, and of the hope, gratitude, love, tenderness, and humiliation, which faith draws therefrom, as means for cultivating repentance.

But in our view it is erroneous to represent faith as existing irrespective of penitence, in its very first acting, and as begetting penitence through the medium of hope. On the contrary, we believe that the very first acting of faith implies some repentance, as the prompter thereof...The man begins to believe because he has also begun to repent.

Godly sorrow for sin must be presupposed or implied in the first actings of faith, because faith embraces Christ as a Saviour from sin...Surely the Scriptures do not present Christ to our faith only, or even mainly, as a way of impunity...As we have pointed out, the most characteristic defect of a dead faith, is, that it would quite heartily embrace Christ as God's provision for immunity in sin: but God offers Him to faith for a very different purpose, viz: for restoration to holiness, including immunity from wrath as one of the secondary consequences thereof.

But now, a man does not flee from an evil, except as a consequence of feeling it an evil. Hence, there can be no embracing of Christ with the heart, as a whole present Saviour, unless sin be felt to be in itself a present evil; and there be a genuine desire to avoid it as well as its penalty...Some passages of Scripture imply the order I have assigned; and I am not aware of any which contradict it. See Mark i.15; Acts ii.38, v.31, xx.21; 2 Tim ii.25.

Repentance and Faith are twin graces, both implicitly contained in the gift of the new heart; and they cannot but co-exist. Repentance is the right sense and volition which the renewed heart has of its sin; faith is the turning of that heart from its sin to Christ. Repentance feels the disease, faith embraces the remedy...The exercise of repentance, while absolutely necessary in all who are saved, creates no atoning merit; and constitutes no ground whatever in justice, why the penitent should have remission of his sins...Repentance is as much a gift of God (Acts v.31), as the remission which it is supposed to purchase...While, therefore, the impenitent cannot be justified, yet the sole ground of justification is the righteousness of Christ imputed to us, and received by faith alone.[72]

B.B. Warfield

By repentance we are to mean, not merely sorrow for and hatred of sin, but also the inward turning away from it to God, with full purpose of new obedience. By original sin we are to mean not merely adherent but also inherent sin, not merely the sinful act of Adam imputed to us, but also the sinful state of our own souls conveyed to us by the just judgment of God. When so understood, it would seem sufficiently clear that we must 'repent of original sin.' The corruption that is derived by us from our first parents comes to us, indeed, as penalty; but it abides in us as sin, and must be looked upon as sin both by God and by enlightened conscience itself...And thus it appears, that so far from its being impossible to repent of original sin, repentance, considered in its normative sense—not as an act of turning away from this sin or that sin, but of turning from sin as such to God—is fundamentally just repentance of 'original sin.' Until we repent of original sin, we have not, properly speaking, repented in the Christian sense at all. For it is characteristic of heathen thought to look upon sin atomistically as only so many acts of sin, and at repentance also, therefore, atomistically as only so many acts of turning away from sinning; the Christian conception probes deeper and finds behind the acts of sin the sinful nature and behind the specific acts of repentance for sins the great normative act of repentance for this sinful nature. He only, then, has really repented who has perceived and felt the filthiness and odiousness of his depraved nature and has turned from it to God with a full purpose of being hereafter more conformed to his image as revealed in the face of Jesus Christ.[73]

John Flavel

No sooner is the soul quickened by the Spirit of God, but it answers, in some measure, the end of God in that work, by its active reception of Jesus Christ, in the way of believing...Nothing but unbelief bars men from Christ and his benefits. As many as (received him); the word signifies 'to accept, take,' or, (as we fitly render it), to receive, assume, or take to us; a word most aptly expressing the nature and office of faith, yea, the very justifying and saving act; and we are also heedfully to note its special object: The text saith not...his, but him, i.e. his person, as he is clothed with his offices, and not only his benefits and privileges. These are secondary and consequential things to our receiving him... **the very essence of saving faith consists in our receiving Christ.**

Christ is offered us in the gospel entirely and undividedly, as clothed with all his offices, priestly, prophetical, and regal; as Christ Jesus the Lord, Acts xv.31, and so the true believer receives him; the hypocrite, like the harlot, is for dividing, but the sincere believer finds the need he hath of every office of Christ, and knows not how to want anything that is in him. His ignorance makes him necessary and desirable to him as a prophet: His guilt makes him necessary as a priest: His strong and powerful lusts and corruptions makes him necessary as a king: and in truth he sees not anything in Christ he can spare; he needs all that is in Christ...Look, **as the three offices are undivided in Christ, so they are in the believer's acceptance;** and before this trial no hypocrite can stand; **for all hypocrites reject and quarrel with something in Christ; they like his pardon better than his government. They call him indeed, Lord and Master, but it is but an empty title they bestow upon him;** for let them ask their own hearts if Christ be Lord over their thoughts, as well as their words; over their secret, as well as open actions; over their darling lusts, as well as others; let them ask, who will appear to be Lord and Master over them, when Christ and the world come in competition?...Surely it is the greatest affront that can be offered to the Divine Wisdom and Goodness, to separate in our acceptance, what is so united in Christ, for our salvation and happiness. **As without any of these offices, the work of our salvation could not be completed, so without acceptance of Christ in them all, our union with him by faith cannot be completed.**

The gospel offer of Christ includes all his offices, and gospel–faith just so receives him; to submit to him, as well as to be redeemed by him; to imitate him in the holiness of life, as well as to reap the purchases and fruits of his death. It must be an entire receiving of the Lord Jesus Christ.

The gospel offers Christ orderly to sinners, first his *person*, then his *privileges*. God first gives his Son, and then with him, or as a consequent of that gift, he gives us all things, Rom viii.32. In the same order must our faith receive him. The believer doth not marry the portion first, and then the person, but to be found in him is the first and great care of a believer...It is the proper order in believing, first to accept the person of the Lord Jesus...**Union with Christ is, in order of nature, antecedent to the communication of his privileges, therefore so it ought to be in the order and method of believing.**...Acceptance, which saith, I take Christ in all his offices to be mine, this fits exactly, and belongs to all true believers...This therefore must be the justifying and saving act of faith...That and no other is the justifying and saving act of faith, to which the properties and effects of saving faith do belong, or in which they are only found...By saving faith, Christ is said to 'dwell in our hearts,' Eph. iii.17, but it is neither by assent, nor assurance, but by acceptance, and receiving him that he dwells in our hearts...By faith we are justified, Rom. v.1...therefore it must be by the receiving act, and no other.

If such a receiving of Christ, as hath been described, be saving and justifying faith, then faith is a work of greater difficulty than most men understand it to be...**It is no easy thing to persuade men to receive Christ as their Lord in all things, and submit their necks to his strict and holy precepts,** though it be a great truth that 'Christ's yoke doth not gall, but grace and adorn the neck that bears it;' that the truest and sweetest liberty is in our freedom from our lusts, not in the fulfilling them; yet who can persuade the carnal heart to believe this? **And much less will men ever be prevailed withal, to forsake father, mother, wife, children, inheritance, and life itself, to follow Christ: and all this upon the account of spiritual and invisible things: and yet this must be done by all that would receive the Lord Jesus Christ upon gospel terms...Many ruin their own souls by** placing the essence of saving faith in naked assent.

See that you receive all Christ, with all your heart. To receive all Christ is to receive his person, clothed with all his offices; and to receive him with all your heart, is to receive him into your understanding, will and affections, Acts viii.37. As there is nothing in Christ that may be refused, so there is nothing in you from which he must be excluded.[74]

John MacArthur

The gospel Jesus proclaimed was a call to discipleship, a call to follow Him in submissive obedience, not just a plea to make a decision or pray a prayer. Jesus' message liberated people from the bondage of their sin while it confronted and condemned hypocrisy. It was an offer of eternal life and forgiveness for repentant sinners, but at the same time it was a rebuke to outwardly religious people whose lives were devoid of true righteousness. It puts shiners on notice that they must turn from sin and embrace God's righteousness. It was in every sense good news, yet it was anything but easy-believism. Our Lord's words about eternal life were invariably accompanied by warnings to those who might be tempted to take salvation lightly. He taught that the cost of following Him is high, that the way is narrow and few find it.

Jesus is both Savior and Lord (Luke 2:1 1), and no true believer would ever dispute that. 'Savior' and 'Lord' are separate offices, but we must be careful not to partition them in such a way that we end up with a divided Christ (cf. I Cor. 1:13). Nevertheless, loud voices from the dispensationalists camp are putting forth the teaching that it is possible to reject Christ as Lord and yet receive Him as Savior. Indeed, there are those who would have us believe that the norm for salvation is to accept Jesus as Savior without yielding to Him as Lord.

We do not 'make' Christ, Lord; He is Lord! Those who will not receive Him as Lord are guilty of rejecting Him. 'Faith' that rejects His sovereign authority is really unbelief. Conversely, acknowledging His lordship is no more a human work than repentance (cf. 2 Tim. 2:25) or faith itself (cf. Eph. 2:8-9). In fact, it is an important element of divinely produced saving faith, not something added to faith...No one who comes for salvation with genuine faith, sincerely believing that Jesus is the eternal, almighty, sovereign God, will willfully reject His authority. True faith is not lip service. Our Lord Himself pronounced condemnation on those who worshipped Him with their lips but not with their lives (Matt. 15:7–9). He does not become anyone's Savior until that one receives Him for who He is—Lord of all (Acts 10:36).

Those who teach that obedience and submission are extraneous to saving faith are forced to make a firm but unbiblical distinction between salvation and discipleship. This dichotomy, like that of the carnal/spiritual Christian, sets up two classes of Christians: believers only, and true disciples. Many who hold this position discard the evangelistic intent of virtually every recorded invitation of Jesus, saying those apply to discipleship, not to salvation...Are we to believe that when Jesus told the multitudes to deny themselves (Luke 14:26), to take up a cross (v. 27), and to forsake all and follow Him (v. 33), His words had no meaning whatsoever for the unsaved people in the crowd?

The call of Calvary must be recognized for what it is: a call to discipleship under the Lordship of Jesus Christ. To respond to that call is to become a believer. Anything less is simply unbelief. The gospel according to Jesus explicitly and unequivocally rules out easy–believism. To make all our Lord's difficult demands apply only to a higher class of Christians blunts the force of His entire message. It makes room for cheap and meaningless faith—a faith that may be exercised with absolutely no impact on the fleshly life of sin. That is not saving faith.[75]

Walter Chantry

Often Christ turned crowds away by insisting that whosoever he be of you that forsaketh not all that he hath, he cannot be my disciple (Luke 14:33). He was not speaking of abundant life nor of 'victorious' giants of the faith. He demanded this turning from everything to Himself as a condition of discipleship for everyone. The young ruler would turn from earthly riches to heavenly or lie would cling to earthly riches and perish. The sinner must know that Jesus will not be a Saviour to any man who refuses to bow to Him as Lord.

Christ knew nothing of the man–made twentieth–century suggestion that taking Jesus as Lord is optional. For Him it was not second step which is essential for great blessings but unnecessary for entering God's kingdom. The altered message of today has deceived men and women by convincing them that Jesus will gladly be a Saviour even to those who refuse to follow Him as Lord. It simply is not the truth! Jesus' invitation to salvation is, 'Come, follow me'. Practical acknowledgments of Jesus' lordship, yielding to His rule by following is the very fibre of saving faith...Believing is obeying. Without obedience, you shall not see life! Unless you bow to Christ's scepter you will not receive the benefits of Christ's sacrifice. That is just what Jesus said to the ruler.[76]

Only one entrance may be found to the kingdom of God. There is a narrow gate set at the head of the path of life. 'Strait is the gate, and narrow is the way, which leadeth unto life, and few there be that find it' (Matt. 7:14). No one with ail inflated ego can squeeze through the door. There must be self–effacement, self–repudiation, self–denial even to become a disciple (a student) of Jesus Christ...Six times in the Gospels our great Prophet refers to His followers taking up a cross. It was one of His favorite illustrations of self-denial.

Some who call themselves 'Christian' in fact have never taken up their crosses. Being ignorant of the experience of self–execution, of self–denial, they are of necessity strangers to Christ. Our Lord Himself intended His illustration and His demand to deepen alarm in such individuals...Without a cross there is no following Christ! And without following Christ there is no life at all! An impression has been given that many enter life through a wide gate of believing on Jesus. Then a few go through the narrow gate of the cross for deeper spiritual service. On the contrary, the broad way without self–denial leads to destruction. All who are saved have entered the fraternity of the cross.[77]

J. C. Ryle

I doubt, indeed, whether we have any warrant for saying that a man can possibly be converted without being consecrated to God!...If he was not consecrated to God in the very day that he was converted and born again, I do not know what conversion means. Are not men in danger of undervaluing and underrating the immense blessedness of conversion? Are they not, when they urge on believers the 'higher life' as a second conversion, underrating the length, and breadth, and depth, and height, of that great first chapter which Scripture calls the new birth, the new creation, the spiritual resurrection? I may be mistaken. But I have sometimes thought, while reading the strong language used by many about 'consecration,' in the last few years, that those who use it must have had previously a singularly low and inadequate view of 'conversions' if indeed they knew anything about conversion at all. In short,

I have almost suspected that when they were *consecrated,* they were in reality *converted* for the first time![78]

John Gerstner

The Church is presently faced with a struggle equal in importance to the fourth century Nicene battle for the deity of Christ and the Reformation struggle for the doctrine of justification by faith. In both of these previous controversies, the very gospel of Jesus Christ was at stake. The situation is no different today. We have shown throughout this volume that Dispensationalism teaches a different gospel. The gospel of dispensational Antinomianism declares that a person may have Christ as Savior but refuses to accept Him as Lord of one's life. This battle has been called the 'Lordship Salvation' controversy.

Without question, the most serious and effective attack on dispensational Antinomianism has come from within dispensational ranks. Though many others had said the same things before him, when John MacArthur, almost universally recognized as a respected dispensationalist himself, wrote *The Gospel According to Jesus,* the fat was in the fire.

The essential declaration of *The Gospel According to Jesus* is that Jesus Himself insists that if a person does not take up Christ's cross and follow Him that person does not have saving faith in Him and will be disowned and damned by Him at the day of judgment. That is shown through parable after parable, teaching after teaching, and illustration after illustration. The appendix adds insult to injury against Dispensationalism's antinomian teaching by showing that the churches historic understanding of the gospel has always recognized the necessity of obedience.

This is no mere ivory tower concern. It is not an esoteric debate among theologians; the antinomian threat is everywhere. Antinomianism has penetrated, and in many cases permeated, many evangelical churches in America. This false gospel is even spread by missionaries in foreign lands...The stakes are indeed high, for the church faces a direct challenge from within Protestantism to the integrity of the gospel message. If Luther had to proclaim to the church of the sixteenth century that justification is by faith alone and not by meritorious works, we must protest to the church, as she approaches the twenty–first century, that justification is by LIVING and not by DEAD faith![79]

Westminster Confession of Faith

The principal acts of saving faith are, accepting, receiving, and resting upon Christ alone for justification, sanctification, and eternal life, by virtue of the covenant of grace (XIV.2).[80]

Repentance unto life is an evangelical grace, the doctrine whereof is to be preached by every minister of the gospel, as well as that of faith in Christ...By it a sinner, out of the sight and sense, not only of the danger, but also of the filthiness and odiousness of his sins, as contrary to the holy nature and righteous law of God, and upon the apprehension of his mercy in Christ to such as are penitent, so grieves for and hates his sins, as to turn from them all unto God, purposing and endeavoring to walk with him in all the ways of his commandments...Although repentance be not to be rested in, as any satisfaction for sin, or any cause of the pardon thereof, which is the act of God's free grace in Christ; yet is it of such necessity to all sinners, that none may expect pardon without it (XV.1,2,3).[81]

[1]J.C. Ryle, *Holiness* (Cambridge:James Clarke & Co.) p. 1

[2]J.I. Packer, *God's Word's* (Downers Grove: Intervarsity, 1981), pp. 72-74.

[3]John Stott, *Basic Christianity* (Grand Rapids: Eerdmans, 1972), pp. 75-78.

[4]Henry Thiessen, *Lectures in Systematic Theology* (Grand Rapids: Eerdmans, 1949), pp. 171-175.

[5]W.E. Vine, *Vine's Expository Dictionary of New Testament Words* (McLean: MacDonald, 1940), p. 657.

[6]Augustus Strong, *Systematic Theology* (Old Tappan: Revell,1907) pp.567-568, 572-573.

[7]Jonathan Edwards, *The Works of Jonathan Edwards* (Edinburgh: Banner, 1974), Volume 2, *Men Naturally Are God's Enemies*, Sect. III, pp. 132-133.

[8]J.I. Packer, *Evangelism and the Sovereignty of God* (Downers Grove:InterVarsity, 1961), p. 70.

[9]*Institutes of the Christian Religion* (Philadelphia: Westminster, 1960), John McNeil, Ed., Volume 1, Book III, Chapter III.1., p. 592.

[10]William Hendriksen, *New Testament Commentary, The Gospel of Luke* (Grand Rapids: Baker, 1978), pp. 734-735.

[11]G. Campbell Morgan, *The Westminster Pulpit*, (Grand Rapids: Baker, 1954) Volume I, pp. 43-44.

[12]William Hendriksen, *New Testament Commentary, The Gospel of Luke* (Grand Rapids: Baker, 1981), p. 737.

[13]John Stott, *Basic Christianity* (Grand Rapids: Eerdmans, 1972), p. 111.

[14]John Stott, *Basic Christianity* (Grand Rapids: Eerdmans, 1972), pp. 111-112.

[15]R.C.H. Lenski, *Interpretation of St. Mark's Gospel* (Minneapolis: Augsburg, 1961), p. 348.

[16]William Hendriksen, *New Testament Commentary, The Gospel of Mark* (Grand Rapids: Baker, 1975), p. 330.

[17]*New Testament Commentary, The Gospel of Luke* (Grand Rapids: Baker, 1978), pp. 498-500).

[18]James Montgomery Boice, *Christ's Call to Discipleship* (Chicago: Moody, 1986), p. 19.

[19]F.F. Bruce, *The Gospel of John* (Grand Rapids: Eerdmans, 1983), p. 265.

[20]D.A. Carson, *The Gospel According to John* (Grand Rapids: Eerdmans, 1991), pp. 438-439.

[21]Walter Chantry, *Today's Gospel - Synthetic or Authentic?* (Edinburgh: Banner, 1970), pp. 55, 59-60.

[22]*The Works of Jonathan Edwards*, Volume 2, Discourse: *Men Naturally are God's Enemies*, pp. 132, 138-139.

[23]J.I. Packer, *Evagelism and the Sovereignty of God* (Downers Grove: InterVarsity, 1961), p. 72.

[24]Henry Thiessen, *Lectures in Systematic Theology* (Grand Rapids: Eerdmans, 1979), pg. 271.

[25]Found in *The Confession of Faith* by A.A. Hodge (Edinburgh: Banner, 1958), p. 204.

[26]*The Works of John Owen* (Edinburgh: Banner, 1965), Volume I, pp. 134, 136.

[27]*Collected Writings of John Murray* (Edinburgh: Banner, 1977), Volume 2, pp. 278-280.

[28]James Montgomery Boice, *Christ's Call to Discipleship* (Chicago: Moody, 1986), pp. 13, 14, 16, 21.

[29]A. W. Tozer, *I Call It Heresy* (Camp Hill:Christian Publications, 1974), pp. 9, 14-16. 18-20.

[30]A.W. Pink, *The Doctrine of Salvation* (Grand Rapids: Baker, 1979), p. 60.

[31]J.C. Ryle, *The Upper Room* (Edinburgh: Banner, 1977), p. 137.

[32]John MacArthur, *Kingdom Living Here and Now* (Chicago: Moody, 1980), pp. 5-22.

[33]R.C.H. Lenski, *Interpretation of St. Matthew's Gospel* (Minneapolis: Augsburg, 1961), pg. 308.

[34]A.W. Tozer, *I Call It Heresy* (Camp Hill: Christian Publications, 1974), p. 20.

[35] A.W. Tozer, *I Call It Heresy* (Camp Hill: Christian Publications, 1974), pp. 9, 14-16, 18-20.

[36] G. Campbell Morgan, *The Westminster Pulpit* (Grand Rapids: Baker, 1954-1955), Vol. 6, pp. 154-166; Vol. 8, p. 121.

[37] J.I. Packer, *Evangelism and the Sovereignty of God* (Downers Grove: InterVarsity, 1961), pp. 38-40, 65, 70-71, 72, 73, 88, 89, 105.

[38] From the Foreword to *The Gospel According to Jesus* (Grand Rapids: Zondervan, 1988) By John MacArthur, p. ix.

[39] John Stott, *Basic Christianity* (Grand Rapids: Eerdmans, 1972), pp. 107-113, 124, 125

[40] D. Martyn Lloyd–Jones, *Studies in the Sermon on the Mount* (Grand Rapids: Eerdmans, 1971), pp. 16, 40, 220, 221, 224, 225, 247, 248.

[41] C. H. Spurgeon, *New Park Street Pulpit*, Vol. 5 and 6, pp. 342-346; Sermon #106, pages 418,419.

[42] C.H. Spurgeon, *The Metropolitan Tabernacle Pulpit*, Vol. 56 (reprint, Pasadena: Pilgrim, 1979), p. 617. Cited by John MacArthur, *Faith Works* (Dallas: Word, 1993), p. 245-246.

[43] Handley Moule, *Practicing the Promises* (Chicago: Moody, 1975), pp. 19-21.

[44] Charles Hodge, *Romans* (Edinburgh: Banner, 1972), p. 341.

[45] Charles Hodge, *Systematic Theology, The Kingly Office of Christ.*

[46] Charles Hodge, *The Way of Life* (Edinburgh: Banner, 1959), pp. 153, 166-169.

[47] Griffith Thomas, *St. Paul's Epistle to the Romans* (Grand Rapids: Eerdmans, 1946, 1974), p. 371.

[48] A.A. Hodge, *Evangelical Theology* (Edinburgh: Banner, 1976), pp. 120, 233.

[49] A.A. Hodge, *Evangelical Theology* (Edinburgh: Banner, 1976), p. 297.

[50] A.W. Pink, *The Doctrine of Salvation* (Grand Rapids: Baker, 1979), pp. 45, 49-53, 56, 58, 60, 79.

[51] James Montgomery Boice, *Christ's Call to Discipleship* (Chicago: Moody, 1986), pp. 13, 14, 16, 21.

[52] William Hendriksen, New Testament Commentary, *The Gospel of Mark* (Grand Rapids: Baker, 1981).

[53] William Hendriksen, New Testament Commentary, *The Gospel of Luke* (Grand Rapids: Baker, 1978), pp. 498-500).

[54] R.C.H. Lenski, *Interpretation of St. Mark's Gospel* (Minneapolis: Augsburg, 1961), p. 348.

[55] John Calvin, *Institutes of the Christian Religion,* John McNeil, Ed., (Philadelphia: Westminster, 1960), Vol. I, Book III, Chapter III. 5-8, pp. 597-600.

[56] D. James Kennedy, *Truths That Transform* (Old Tappan:Revell, 1974), pp. 63-66.

[57] J.B. Lightfoot, *St. Paul's Epistles to the Colossians and to Philemon* (Grand Rapids: Zondervan, 1959), p. 121.

[58] Henry Thiessen, *Lectures in Systematic Theology* (Grand Rapids: Eerdmans, 1979), pp. 268-270, 271-273.

[59] Augustus H. Strong, *Systematic Theology* (Old Tappan: Revell, 1907), pp. 829, 832-836.

[60] Louis Berkhof, *Systematic Theology* (Grand Rapids: Eerdmans, 1939), pp. 503-505

[61] Louis Berkhof, *Systematic Theology* (Grand Rapids: Eerdmans, 1939), p 506.

[62] Louis Berkhof, *Systematic Theology* (Grand Rapids: Eerdmans, 1939), p. 492.

[63] *Collected Writings of John Murray* (Edinburgh: Banner, 1977), Volume 2, pp.257-260.

[64] *Collected Writings of John Murray* (Edinburgh: Banner, 1977), Volume 2, pp. 220-221.

[65] *Collected Writings of John Murray* (Edinburgh: Banner, 1977), Volume 2, pp. 169-170.

[66] *Collected Writings of John Murray* (Edinburgh: Banner, 1977), Volume 2, pp. 216-217.

[67] *Collected Writings of John Murray* (Edinburgh: Banner, 1977), Volume 2, p. 217.

[68] R.L. Dabney, *Systematic Theology* (Edinburgh: Banner, 1871) p. 601, 658, 664.

[69] R.L. Dabney, *Systematic Theology* (Edinburgh: Banner, 1871) p. 606-607.

[70] R.L. Dabney, *Systematic Theology* (Edinburgh: Banner, 1871) p. 600.

[71] R.L. Dabney, *Systematic Theology* (Edinburgh: Banner, 1871) p. 607.

[72] R.L. Dabney, *Systematic Theology* (Edinburgh: Banner, 1871), pp. 651, 654, 656-659.

[73] B.B. Warfield, *Selected Shorter Writings–1* (Nutley: Presbyterian & Reformed, 1970), pp. 279-280.

[74] *John Flavel* (Edinburgh: Banner, 1968), Volume 2, pp. 102-105, 107-112, 115, 122-123, 140.

[75] John MacArthur, *The Gospel According to Jesus* (Grand Rapids: Zondervan, 1988), pp. 21-33.

[76] Walter Chantry, *Today's Gospel: Authentic or Synthetic?* (Edinburgh: Banner, 1970), pp. 59-60.

[77] Walter Chantry, *The Shadow of the Cross* (Edinburgh: Banner), pp. 19-20, 22.

[78] J.C. Ryle, *Holiness* (Cambridge: James Clark), p. 57.

[79] John Gerstner, *Wrongly Dividing the Word of Truth* (Brentwood: Wolgemuth & Hyatt, 1991), pp. 251-253, 258-259.

[80] Found in *The Confession of Faith* by A.A. Hodge (Edinburgh: Banner, 1958), p. 204.

[81] Found in *The Confession of Faith* by A.A. Hodge (Edinburgh: Banner, 1958), pp. 210-213.